RECOVERING FROM THE TRAUMA OF ADDICTION

TEENA CLIPSTON, PAM RADER, LUKE WILTSHIRE,
BRENDA-LYNN HALEY, HEATHER ALEXANDER, DAWN FINN,
DANNA BUSHELL, AND SPECIAL GUEST AUTHORS.

published by Clipston Publishing
www.clipstonpublishing.com

Healing Mind, Body, & Soul: Recovering from the Trauma of Addiction
Copyright © 2024 Clipston Publishing
First Edition: September 2024.

All rights reserved. No part of this publication may be reproduced, distributed, or transmitted in any form or by any means, including photocopying, recording, or other electronic or mechanical methods, without the prior written permission of the publisher, Clipston Publishing, except in the case of brief quotations embodied in critical reviews, academic use, or certain other non-commercial purposes permitted by copyright law.

Compilation Notice:
This book is a compilation of individual contributions from various authors, for which Clipston Publishing holds the first publishing rights. The publisher retains the collective copyright for this compilation. No part of this compilation, including individual contributions, may be reproduced without the express written consent of Clipston Publishing.

Limitation of Liability:
Under no circumstances shall Clipston Publishing, its affiliates, editors, or contributing authors be liable for any indirect, incidental, consequential, special, or exemplary damages arising out of or in connection with your use of any healing recommendations or information contained in this book. The information and suggestions presented in the text are for informational purposes only and are not intended as a substitute for professional medical, mental health, or legal advice. Readers should consult a licensed professional before undertaking any actions related to health or lifestyle changes. The views, thoughts, and opinions expressed by the authors belong solely to them and do not necessarily reflect those of Clipston Publishing, its editorial team, or other contributors.

Published by Clipston Publishing
Edited by Rusti L Lehay and Virginia L Lehay
Design and layout by Teena Clipston

ISBN: 978-1-7381705-1-7 (Print)
ISBN: 978-1-7381705-2-4 (eBook)

Ordering Information:
Special discounts are available for quantity purchases by corporations, associations, and educational institutions. For more information, please contact Teena Clipston at teena@clipstonpublishing.com. Programs, products, or services offered by the individual authors may be accessed by contacting them directly.

www.clipstonpublishing.com

The stories in this book are raw, real, and unfiltered. We commend the authors for their courage in sharing their experiences.

"Your story is the key to unlocking someone else's future." – Unknown

Content Notice

Warning: This book contains discussions of drug use, addiction, and related issues, which may include graphic depictions of violence, emotional distress, and other sensitive subjects. The content is intended for mature readers and may not be suitable for all ages. Reader discretion is advised.

Disclaimer

The content of this book is provided for informational and inspirational purposes only. The stories shared are personal accounts and reflections of the authors. While they offer valuable insights, they do not constitute medical, psychological, or professional advice. The publisher and authors do not guarantee the accuracy or completeness of the information and are not responsible for any actions taken based on the content of this book.

Readers are encouraged to seek professional guidance for issues related to addiction, mental health, or any other concerns addressed in this book. The experiences and recommendations shared are individual and may not apply to everyone.

To ensure the safety of the authors and their families, some names have been changed and certain details have been omitted.

 EDICATION

To my son, Andrew, who overcame the darkness of opioid addiction and survived the impossible. Your strength and resilience inspire me every day, and it is with your courage and approval that I am able to share our story with readers, in the hope that it helps other parents and their children lost to the opioid crisis.

And to those who did not survive—your lives mattered, and your battles will never be forgotten. And to those still fighting, may this book offer you the hope and strength to continue on your journey toward recovery.

With deepest gratitude,
Teena Clipston

Table of Contents

Foreword by Guy Felicella..01
Editor's Note by Rusti L Lehay..05

Stories:

  Surrendering to Love in the Face of Addiction
  by Pam Rader..11

  Catalyst of Conscience
  by Luke Wiltshire 23

  The Trauma Landscape
  by Danna Bushell...33

  A Journey of Recovery and Transformation
  by Dawn Finn...45

  Wildflower: An Unfinished Love Story
  by Anne Theriault...55

  Everything is (Not) Normal
  by Heather Alexander..65

  It Ain't No Movie
  by Callum Roth 77

  In the World of an Indian Woman
  by Yiktsa7: Carol Thevarge 89

  Guerrilla Grands
  by Alma Lee Byzewski..101

  Chasing Symptoms
  by Brenda-Lynn Haley..109

  Dark Castle
  by Ben Goerner 117

Pecking Order
by Helena Paivinen 127
From ~~Junkie~~, ~~Addict~~, ~~Criminal~~, and ~~Ex-Con~~ to Captain Hamish
by Hamish Roth 135
Lost Girl
by Stacy Zeman..145
Living Proof of the Maverick Protocol
by Taylor Pridy 155
Saving My Son
by Teena Clipston..167

Community letters 181
   The Core Centre for Health 183
   ASK Wellness Society..185
   John Howard Society of British Columbia 189
   Alberta Adolescent Recovery Centre 191
   Ki-Low-Na Frienship Society..195
   Sena College of Massage Therapy.......................................199

Resources 201
   Canada & USA: Addiction Recovery Resources..................203
   Canada & USA: Addiction Rehab Centres 207

Acknowledgments 213

Foreword

by Guy Felicella

As someone who spent decades homeless, addicted, in and out of jail, barely surviving life-threatening infections that nearly took my leg and left me unable to walk, I was once considered a "hopeless case" in Vancouver's notorious Downtown East Side. I was entrenched in a three-block radius, and no amount of detox or treatment changed the trajectory of my life. Instead, services in the Downtown East Side started to adapt programs around users like me to prevent overdoses and limit the spread of infectious diseases. From there, facilities like Insite, North America's first safe consumption site, were born. Today, I dedicate my time passionately and fiercely advocating for harm reduction services. The same ones that kept me breathing when my choices put me on a fast track to six feet under.

Today, I am a sought-after international public speaker, advocate, writer, educator, and expert on addiction, harm reduction, and recovery. I speak worldwide at conferences, community events, secondary schools, universities, and government agencies. My testament to the resilience of the human spirit is valuable. I harness my career and platform to advocate tirelessly for crucial causes such as trauma therapy, harm reduction, swifter access to treatment, and reformed drug policies. I stand as a beacon of inspiration for countless individuals who have faced similar trials and tribulations and push for a more compassionate and effective approach to drug policy and addiction treatment.

This is why, when Teena asked me to be a part of this important project, I couldn't resist an opportunity to invigorate hope into the hearts of people who are struggling with or love someone who is struggling with addiction. I grew up in a middle-class Italian/German home. From the outside looking in, it appeared that I was raised in a "good family" but from the inside, we lived in a pattern of dysfunction, abuse, and addiction. As the oldest of three and with undiagnosed ADHD, I received the brunt of the abuse and negative attention. This negativity, mixed with the scrutiny I received at school for my poor performance and behaviour, led me to adopt the belief that I was stupid, worthless, and unwanted which led to self-hatred, anxiety, and depression. To escape those feelings, I fell into the thrill and adrenaline found in crime, gangs, and drugs.

I became a ward of the court and spent my teenage years bouncing through foster care until I eventually found myself homeless, addicted, and entrenched in the Downtown East Side. After a childhood of feeling rejected and discarded, I finally felt like I was "home" in a community of people who felt the same way. Like many, I cycled through jails, treatment facilities, and the street, barely escaping the multiple health crises that affected the city. When fentanyl hit the streets, I overdosed multiple times in one year, with my last overdose lasting over six minutes. I was brought back to life by a nurse at Insite and realized that I was either going to die or die trying to get out.

It was here that I found myself at 43, with one set of clothes, determined to restart my life. I rekindled a relationship with my now-wife, and together we built from the ground up. I got my bank account, identification, and driver's license back. I paid off old debts, got a job, and started a family. I bought a house, started a career with Vancouver Coastal Health, and auditioned for my first TEDx Talk. Today, I'm a father of three and have over a decade of recovery. Every day, I wake up humbled by my second chance at life.

Sadly, the unregulated toxic drug supply is the number one leading cause of death among people aged 10-59 in British Columbia. Many people do not receive a second chance. Just as deadly as the drugs themselves, the stigma that surrounds addiction is causing people to use alone, increasing their chances of fatal overdoses. Stigma around addiction creates more than a difficult choice for people to reach out for help. It is a mile-high barrier as they fear and risk losing their housing, job, children, family, or friends while receiving harsh judgment and discrimination. They often struggle silently and try to hold it all together on their own. Parents have shared their own experiences with feeling isolated and devalued after sharing that their child is struggling with addiction.

That is why this book is so vital in changing the narrative around addiction. Addiction doesn't discriminate; it impacts all races, genders, and ages world-wide, from doctors to professional athletes to people living in poverty. There is no socioeconomic class, profession, or status that addiction doesn't infiltrate.

Why? Addiction is driven by pain. People with unhealed pain and trauma often succumb to disastrous coping mechanisms to escape. Without proper support, it will continue to negatively impact people's lives and be passed down through generational cycles. It's important to remember that everyone has a story. When looking at addiction, we need to understand the story behind the person. Somewhere inside that person lives shame, low self-worth, abandonment, fear, sadness, and rejection, all stemming from unresolved trauma.

When we view addiction through a lens of compassion and human connection, people get better. When we offer people support and services that affirm that their lives have value, they get better. When we meet people with empathy and non-judgment when they reach out for help, people get better. When people share their stories and inspire others to keep going, like they have in this book, people get better.

When I was homeless, sleeping in a doorway, or laying on an injection site floor being revived from my sixth overdose, people didn't believe I would get better, but the kindness and compassion I received from others when I was at my worst kept me going.

Harm reduction kept me alive, human connection kept my spirit hungry, and recovery gave me the tools and support that I needed to build the life and family I have today. I believe this book will inspire, encourage, and change the direction of other people's lives. Keep believing!

Guy Felicella
www.guyfelicella.com

It Takes A Village

Editor's Note

by Rusti L Lehay

From a freak misfire of a well-maintained 9mm pistol to divine intervention, astral travel, and the pecking order of children bullying one author mercilessly in her childhood, I kept a hanky close for all the tears of awe I shed. Empathy flowed along with compassion and respect for these authors. Some of them have never written anything for print before, and now you have their words on these pages, offering their raw, completely honest, slices of life that most of us never come close to experiencing. Their journeys to uncover the staunchest resilience, the deepest self-forgiveness, and the utmost drive to serve others in the trenches where they once almost died are beyond remarkable. In fact, several of these authors brushed into death's hallways more than once, being resuscitated again and again.

You will witness the phenomenal love of the mothers, fathers, stepfathers, and siblings who keep the family ties open with boundaries that support without abandonment. Be prepared to weep along with the mother imagining how to write a eulogy for her wildflower daughter, and the mother who did lose her son to substance abuse, squashing their joint dream to work in the recovery field together. Understand the trauma landscape incurred by the families and parents who suffer complex and chronic post-traumatic stress disorder which is linked as an underlying cause for many health conditions. How can you expect a parent watching their child cavort with death again and again to not be traumatized? You cannot.

Join me in awe as one mother learned to ask herself, "What does it look like just to love him?" With great humility, she apologized for making him wrong to be an addict. Like magic, her son, who used to blame everyone, embraced accountability. This may have been one of the pivotal moments where he stepped onto the recovery path. This mother and son now enjoy each other in a way that had been unimaginable for over a decade.

Be inspired by one Guerrilla Grand standing up to law enforcement authorities. Emergency room patients applauded this grandmother when she cited the law to a police officer. She insisted charges would be laid or that the domestic violence special constable would face an inquiry and possibly be out of work by morning. The grandmother knew the law codes. Learn how she used decorative gravel to protect her grandchild and how, to another author, the crunch of tires on gravel signified the possibility of impending abuse and the need to be tiny and disappear.

Celebrate with the First Nations woman who, after watching so many of her family members die from suicide, overdose, or accidents, recovered her own sobriety. She put her children first over a relationship, and now mentors others to learn and reclaim cultural customs and how to harvest traditional herbs with medicinal properties.

Then there are the unknown yet not forgotten street angels who work tirelessly to bring people back from the dead and free them from paranoia and drug-induced psychosis that takes over so many. One outreach volunteer for the homeless called a mother to say, "Your son needs you. I don't know if he will survive." Then drove the young man, nearly a stranger, and certainly she was to him in his drug-induced psychosis, between cities to reunite this author with her son. Together, they healed old wounds and found joy in shared sunsets and the wider beauty of life.

There is awe, danger, and scenes like gangster movies glorifying the drug culture in these stories that illuminate the bare bones of the dark truths of addiction. Though the life of one author became more like a horror movie when he was beaten and threatened with a chainsaw. From darkness to light, each one of these authors drilled gratitude into my core for my sheltered farmgirl, prairie life. While I was saving pennies, dimes, babysitting, and egg money to leave small-town rural Alberta, many of these authors were surviving, not thriving, on the streets of our bigger cities dealing, buying, and getting high until there was no place higher and all they could do was plummet into the abyss of addiction. Plummet they did like one author who never ventured outside of a six-block radius of Vancouver's Main Street and Hastings. After 18 treatment centres, suffering lung collapses from infection and told by his parents, "We can't continue watching you die," this author survived and now thrives. He is now a senior captain living on a small island with a woman he loves.

Redemption and recovery are there if we only look. Methadone has become readily available in drug stores on a prescription basis. Although this method of harm reduction is not the holy grail, it provides an important beginning to recovery for some. For one author, he felt methadone was only another stigmatized addiction. He now works tirelessly to promote how recovery programs demanding absolute abstinence before treatment is an unrealistic expectation. Safety, relief from dope sickness, basic respect, nutrition, family support, and shelter are essential steps to be implemented early on the twisted path to full sobriety.

Even though I grew up around alcohol abuse and watched cousins flirt with drugs, I maintained a distance, possibly because I was already an outcast and didn't fit into any group. While my mother preached to the preteen and teenager me on all the ways to avoid pregnancy, one author, a teen mom at 15, independently put herself through high school. She used a sleigh and a stroller to pick up bottles and cans for their deposits to purchase extra diapers and healthier food when social assistance barely covered utilities, food, and rent. To provide a safe home for her infant, she left the child's father, whom she loved, when he was dealing.

To those of you who had a sheltered life or never had to deal with trauma so large that substances were the only way to cope when society, school, and trusted coaches failed them, I say, "Sit up. Pay attention. See the person and the pain behind the mask of the high." Trauma work, healing from trauma, preventing trauma, and safeguarding our youth are just a few of the steps needed as a first line of defence. Then compassion and respect with informed and up-to-date harm reduction services, sites, and supplies. As Guy Felicella says in the foreword, addiction spares no class or level of society. One author, a professional educator, dealing with debilitating pain all her life, counted up having taken 35,000 of "the least addictive of the opioid" pills her doctor deemed safe. That number doesn't even touch all the other medical prescriptions she took on a daily basis. Readers will see how she freed herself with the support of her village.

To further debate how substance use can infiltrate at every level of society and how we need to pay more attention to our youth, one author grew up in a home environment that appeared "normal" in all ways we might define average family life. As a highly sensitive child, growing up in the absence of demonstrative love, acceptance, and validation, she didn't feel human. In high school, she found the other kids in pain and started smoking pot every day. The rest of her story is unique and yet the same, as all the stories in this book share their pain, sorrows, and some make it through while tragically, others do not.

Dear reader, if you are one of the many out there currently struggling with substance abuse, it is my deep hope that these authors will inspire you to take your first steps towards recovery. Breathe in that fresh oxygen of hope, be inspired by how you can walk the recovery road, and keep on walking to reach your first, second, third year cake, and beyond. You are stronger than the chemicals, stronger than the pain, especially once you find that one person who can see you, the one who will sit still with you in the silence and hold space for you in the grief that addiction brings after the highs. There are sunsets to explore, sunrises to see, and many more roads to travel with the feather lightness of being that true freedom can bring. No mountain is high enough to surpass the intensity of truly loving yourself. Many of these authors share how self-love played an integral part in their sobriety.

Witness these authors who reach for recovery, empathize with the parents and loved ones who find a way to support and love throughout the twisted journey of addiction, mourn those who lost the battle, and celebrate with all those who have recovered. Show gratitude and awe for those who now serve out there on the front lines, doing their part to support people on the perilous road to recovery. One person can make a difference. Together, we can change the world. What can you do?

For starters, read this book and see others and yourself with different eyes.

Sincerely,

Rusti L Lehay

Surrendering to Love in the Face of Addiction

by Pam Rader

All the air seems to leave the room as I struggle to comprehend the words that unintentionally assault my ears. Just moments before, I had been leaning against my dining room chair with a steaming cup of herbal tea in my hand, relaying plans to travel to Vancouver to visit friends. The fragility of the peace I've cultivated in my life is now suddenly exposed with the utterance of one simple sentence.

"You will be bringing your son home with you."

The joy of spending a weekend with my closest friends dissolves in the heaviness that descends over my body. The familiar cold, black fist of fear rises from its storage locker in the basement of my belly. I consider what my trusted spiritual teacher has just offered in his matter-of-fact way. I feel a little like the wind has been knocked out of me, and it takes me a moment to respond, "I think you're mistaken; Nick is in a treatment center. I won't take him out of rehab to bring him home. It's too much chaos in our house and our lives if he's using."

Joe, also known as Foxdreamer, lifts his piercing blue eyes from the mug of tea nestling between his hands. Those eyes always surprise me, no matter how often I see them. Blue eyes peering out from his indigenous features and salt and pepper hair give Joe a unique and powerful presence. "Are you sure about that? They are showing me that you will be bringing him home and that I am supposed to tell you it's important."

As a Native Medicine Man, Joe has been instrumental in expanding my knowledge of spirituality and energy. The visions he's shared with me over the past year have all come to fruition. The "they" he refers to are the spirits, guides, and angels that Joe has been a conduit for during his life. I hear his words yet struggle to comprehend the implications. Does this mean Nick's not in treatment? If he's not in rehab, where is he? Here we go again. I don't know if I have it in me to do this one more time. Treatment gives me 60 to 90 days of regular sleep. He's barely been there for two weeks. I let out an audible sigh.

"Are you sure? I really don't think so, Joe..." Hope and fear mingled in my voice. Maybe this time he's wrong.

He nods his head downward toward his mug, and one corner of his mouth turns up in a half-smile. "We'll see."

Nicholas has been in and out of drug treatment centres and detox facilities dozens of times. At 29 years old, he has spent half of his life battling a merciless addiction that is unmatched even by his biological father's alcoholism, which eventually took his life. My once sweet, smart, and sassy boy has now been reduced to a life of shame, devastation, and hopelessness, interrupted by the occasional respite and faint hope that another treatment centre provides.

If you've ever braced for a fall, you know that it doesn't make the fall hurt any less. You are more likely to get injured if you try to prevent the impact. My first husband, Nick's father, who had the propensity to drink a bottle of vodka before driving the winding highway to work, was thrown over 100 meters from his vehicle after falling asleep at the wheel and swerving into an embankment. When he arrived at the hospital, I expected catastrophic injuries, but all he had was a bad case of road rash. Drunks don't brace.

Unfortunately, when you aren't equipped with the necessary tools, all you can do is brace. I prayed daily for years on end that my son would be spared the horrors of addiction. I prayed he wouldn't go down the path that led his father to try to murder me and ultimately land him in prison. I didn't know any other way to do it. When my prayers failed, I took matters into my own hands. I tried to control it.

The need for control, like addiction, is akin to a nuclear bomb. It doesn't just annihilate its target; it devastates everything in its path. Nick's addiction to drugs continued to spiral out of control while my need to try to control both him and my life escalated at an identical pace. My son's drug of choice was fentanyl, while my drug of choice was control. No matter how much I braced, the punches kept landing.

Years ago, the discovery of the IV needle carelessly discarded under his bed sent me into a despair I had never felt before. I thought that ugly little syringe would be the nail in both our coffins. I was down-to-my-bones kind of weary. Battling against reality had sapped my vitality and left me hollow and helpless. Just because I thought my son shouldn't be an addict didn't make it so. In my need to control everything when life seemed so out of my control, I made his addiction, and subsequently, my son, the enemy.

The sight of the needle had changed everything. My energy had been focused on all the wrong things. Until I saw the needle, I hadn't dared to ask myself what was most important to me—what did I want? What could I control?

The needle forced me to ask a new question: what would matter most if today was my son's last day on earth? The answer was clear and resounding. I wanted him to know he was loved, to feel seen, heard, and known, and to know that he didn't have to be different to be worthy of my love.

If I were going to march toward peace in my heart, I had to do something different. I needed to lay down the weapons of anger and indignation. I would have to stop making my son wrong for being an addict. I would have to give up my obsession with trying to control something much bigger than both of us.

There is nothing like the fear of losing someone to put life into perspective. I would have to take out the trash to bring forth the love I wanted to share. It turns out that "the trash" wasn't my son's addiction but my attitude about it. It was time for surrender.

I adopted a mantra that guided me through the next several years. "What does it look like just to love him?"

This question gave me access to a new way of being.

When I was raging against a perceived enemy, the inevitable result was anger and division. When I acted from love, new opportunities began to arise. In addiction recovery, addicts are guided to make amends to those they have harmed through their addiction. The trauma of loving an addict had turned me into something I never wanted to be. I had amends of my own to make.

My hands trembled, and my heart hammered inside my chest as I made the call. I knew it was the right thing to do, but I had no idea what the outcome would be. My relationship with Nick could be volatile, but I was committed to starting my healing journey.

"Hey, Mom," his voice sounded tired. I closed my eyes and took a deep breath.

"Nick, I have something important to say, and I would love it if you would just listen. I don't expect anything from you, but I need to say something…" I plowed on… "I apologize for making you wrong for being an addict. It must be so difficult to wake up every day and have to battle addiction while having your mom, the person who is supposed to love you most in the world, make you wrong at every turn. I can't imagine how hard this has all been for you. Can you forgive me?"

A long silence ensued, followed by a minor miracle. "Mom, there is nothing to forgive. I am alive because of you. I don't know where I would be if it weren't for you fighting for me. I am in this predicament because of my choices, and you aren't responsible for any of this. I am."

Up until that point, Nick had blamed everyone and everything around him for his struggles. He had never taken responsibility for anything. I had witnessed him stealing money from my wallet with my own eyes, only to have him tell me that I was crazy and seeing things. It turns out that taking responsibility is contagious. When I cleaned up my side of the street, it opened up space for a new conversation.

I learned to ask myself, "What does it look like just to love him?"

When I was scared, frustrated, or angry, I repeated the question, "What does it look like just to love him?"

Sometimes, just loving him required that I uphold a boundary so I wouldn't feel taken advantage of. I learned that when you have to choose between guilt and resentment, it's better to feel guilty for saying "no" and upholding a boundary than feel resentful for allowing it to fall. It's impossible to be both loving and resentful at the same time.

Sometimes, just loving him meant stifling a sob when he told me he had been hit over the head with a brick and robbed by drug dealers. When everything in me wanted to rush to his aid, I would say, "I'm sorry that happened to you. I love you."

Sometimes, just loving him was knowing when to hang up the phone so an unnecessary argument couldn't ensue. Most of the time, I just listened and reminded myself that there was nothing to fix and that my only job was to love him.

Nick tried to get clean dozens of times, though at first, it was more due to a lack of options than any sort of readiness. The cycle became familiar. He ran out of pavement and had nowhere to go, so he'd go to treatment. A few weeks or, if we were lucky, a few months later, I could predict the relapse; it was as reliable as a Swiss watch. There was something in his tone that I could always detect about a week before he relapsed, and the cycle would start all over again. Each time, it was devastating, but each relapse reminded me that addiction is a lifetime disease and sobriety is not a linear path. I noticed myself recovering from the devastation of each relapse with a little more grace. Acceptance and surrender helped me to reclaim my life. I worked to heal myself. I dove into practicing and teaching yoga and meditation. I worked hard on my marriage and the relationships with my other three children. I let go of what I couldn't control and put my efforts into what I could. I started to experience interludes of peace.

Addiction is progressive. No one with a substance abuse disorder escapes that reality. As Nick's addiction and his circumstances continued to worsen, our relationship remained strong.

Now that I wasn't trying to control the outcome, I could simply show up in our relationship with love. I accepted that recovery would be his journey if he were to find it.

Despite all of my efforts, I realize that acceptance is not a permanent state; it's a moment-by-moment practice. There have been moments of total acceptance, followed by a return to the desire to rail against the reality of my son's addiction. My acceptance has been tested with Joe's words; an old, familiar dread struck fresh into my heart. It's one thing "just to love him" when he's living in another city. It's far more challenging to remain peaceful and loving when he's shooting up in my bathroom and calling dealers in the middle of the night.

My husband and I made the trip to Vancouver and tried to put Joe's words out of our minds. Though the undercurrent of Joe's statement hums like an electrical current in the background, we do our best to push aside what is starting to feel like an inevitable and potentially devastating disruption to our lives. Though the weekend is full of laughter, love, and food, I feel the weight of a stone at the bottom of my stomach. As we depart on the four-hour drive home, I allow myself to do what I've been putting off all weekend. The phone feels heavier than usual, and three rings seem like an eternity, especially for a treatment center. *Why don't they answer right away?* I must get past the lump in my throat; I swallow hard when the receptionist answers the call. "This is Pam Rader; I am Nick's mother. May I speak with him, please?"

A long pause followed, "Can you hold a minute?"

I now know what my pounding heart was trying to tell me. It is unnecessary to hear the supervisor's words, "I am sorry to tell you, but Nick was discharged two days ago. He was caught using drugs, and we had to let him go."

My husband, Chris, has been a part of Nick's life since my son was 12. None of this is new to him. He sees the look on my face and wraps his arms around me. "I'm so sorry, baby." We put smiles on so as not to drag everyone down. Later, my friend from high school, Gillian, gave me a knowing look that said, *"I love you, and I'm sorry, and I'm here no matter what."* It's astounding what 35 years of friendship can do for your telepathy skills.

As we get into the car, Joe's words ring in my ears and I am terrified and angry. When is this going to end? I feel an unravelling from deep within. Have I been fooling myself? I try calling the last number that I have for Nick, and it goes straight to voice mail, causing a mixture of terror and relief. I guess we are heading home. Maybe Joe was wrong. A ding on my phone alerts me to a new social media message. I glance at it, and my heart resumes its gallop. "Hey Mom, it's me. I'm at a store in the mall using their display tablet to message you. My phone is gone. Can you pick me up?"

I'm heartbroken, scared, and I'm pissed off. *He's going to hijack my life... again...why can't he get it together? It's easier to love you from a distance, Nick... Not seeing you running the streets in our town has given me some normalcy...* Mixed in, Joe's words keep playing in my mind; apparently, my resolve will be tested. My husband glances at the message and nods. I texted Nick back, "We are on our way."

My anger dissolves as I take in the sorrowful sight that awaits me. My usually handsome and strapping son is emaciated; his 6-foot frame is stooped, his face sunken and full of scabs. His black hoodie looks two sizes too big, and his black sweatpants badly need washing. It's raining, and he's drenched. I notice a black garbage bag sitting by the curb, containing what I assume are the last of his possessions. Both Chris and I took one look at him and knew that Joe was right.

We arrive home and go through the well-choreographed act of setting out the boundaries. Nick is respectful and subdued as we help him get settled, but it was clear on the drive that something was different. Nick has always had a brilliant mind. He is usually observant, funny, and savvy. Today, he's paranoid and irrational. His mind is failing him. Is it psychosis? Chris takes me aside, "He's completely fucked up. He can't be on his own at this point. But he can't stay here if he's using. Can we try to get him in somewhere else?" Nick agrees that treatment is the necessary next step and willingly makes the calls to start the process again.

The next few days mostly go as expected. When Nick is around, manipulating and lying are well-tread paths, but something is distinctly different. "Mom, get down!!! Close the blinds. Remember those guys I told you were after me? They bugged my phone. They know I'm here. They are coming to kill me."

The bouts of paranoia are worsening. I know I can't control what's happening, but I can do what I can to care for myself and hold space for my son. I call Joe.

The doorbell rings, and Joe and his partner Cindy stand ready with Joe's case, which contains his traditional smudge medicines. He prepares the smudge and extracts a massive eagle feather from his case. Nick appears smaller than usual, with his eyes sunken and his skin grey. He sits quietly in the armchair at the end of the dining room table while Joe concocts the blend of sage and herbs he will use in his energy clearing. I have no illusions about the ritual suddenly making my son well. I called Joe because he has a calming effect on me, and I pray that his energy will have the same impact on my son. Joe's hands are steady, one wielding the eagle feather and the other hovering over Nick's head.

"Nick, call in your guides and angels and ask them to help you, okay?" Nick nods off in a fentanyl-induced haze. Joe glances up at me with bright eyes and a surprised smile. He turns to his partner, Cindy.

"Whoa, I haven't seen this many angels in a long time. You've got a lot of spirits helping you, Nick."

Nick perks up slightly.

"I see a change. Things are going to change for you. You are going to help a lot of people. There is a girl. She's good. She will help. Pray to meet the girl who is going to help." There is a long pause while the smudging and energy clearing continues. "Have you been to the other side, Nick?"

Nick nods. "I've OD'd quite a few times."

Joe nods. "They are showing me that you've been to the other side. They also showed me a baby swaddled in a blanket and handed it to you."

I had never dared to dream of a life where my son was well and had a child.

Nick thanks Joe and Cindy and removes himself to our guestroom. Joe advises me to let him sleep. "He has a lot of healing to do. There are repairs that he needs to make with you and with his grandmother. Healing is happening. He has a choice to make; if he makes the right one, he will be okay. He just has to decide." Joe has first-hand experience as a former addict himself, and something in me trusts that it's going to be okay. I dare to let a glimmer of hope enter my heart.

Eventually, the call we've been waiting for comes in. The local treatment facility in Kelowna can admit Nick in two days. I can leave town to lead my yoga retreat in Spain without worry.

I pack my bags and ask my husband and family to check on Nick while I'm gone. As I board the plane, I text Chris, "If something happens when I'm gone, don't tell me." If I am distracted by what's happening at home, I won't be able to deliver the quality retreat my attendees have come to respect. It feels like a betrayal, but I do it anyway.

When I returned from Spain, I was crushed to learn that Nick had been living in a tent in the bush for most of the time I was away. I am sickened and devastated. He lasted a week in treatment before he relapsed. The relapses are happening faster, and the stints of sobriety are getting shorter. This is bad. My family has made sure he has a phone and that he is fed and has necessities, but his psychosis has been persistent, and his fading grip on reality makes it impossible for him to stay with anyone.

My heart knows that the time is near. He can't live like this for long. It's life or death. I pray for the strength to accept the inevitable call telling me that my son is gone.

The Power of One More Chance
Nicholas is relaxed and as happy as I've ever seen him. We chat and laugh together in a way I never dared to dream possible. "Mom, I never thought I could have a life like this," he beams. He is not just surviving; he is thriving. He has been clean and sober for 16 months, and he has a beautiful girlfriend that we all adore, a puppy named Teddy, and a career as a sought-after barber. He is an integral part of a transformative sober-living community in New Westminister; I hear many express what a good friend he is to them.

It's nothing short of a miracle.

His strength, courage, and resilience deeply humble me. Even when he was at his worst, something in him kept fighting. Every time he fell, he got back up. The healthcare experts who deemed him hopeless had offered him harm reduction. They would enrol him in a program that would allow him to be injected with morphine twice a day to manage his addiction. Nick still had some fight in him and said, "Don't give up on me."

But how did he get here? Even I don't know the answer.

I asked Nick, "You've been to treatment dozens of times. What was different this time?" He pensively looked down at his shoes, and a furrow formed on his brow, and a reflective pause ensued.

He raised his gaze, and the left corner of his mouth turned up. "I asked a new question."

After five weeks of attending a last-chance treatment center known for its strict policies and decent success rates, my son was kicked out of treatment yet again for relapsing. Homeless and hopeless, Nick tried to process what seemed like his inevitable future: street life, overdose, and death. Watching life go by from a park bench with drugs as his only companion, he was despondent. He had reached a point where he no longer cared if he lived or died. Indifference is the most dangerous place to be as an addict.

Alone, ashamed, and contemplating the sweet relief of death, Nick's trajectory was interrupted by a passerby. A young man acquainted with Nick through the recovery community came across him in the park. "Hey man, I thought you were in treatment. What happened?"

"I relapsed." No reasons, no excuses. Nick was done with explanations.

His friend could see the situation was dire. "It's not over yet. Have you heard what Ronnie and Lara are doing down the street? They have a recovery house where you might have a real shot at getting clean and having a life. If I talk to Ronnie, would you be willing to give it a shot?"

"I guess I've got nothing to lose."

Nick's first meeting with Ronnie offered a possible sliver of redemption. He had nowhere left to go. Ronnie, in recovery for more than 15 years, was passionate about helping others, and he seemed different to Nick somehow.

Ronnie wouldn't take Nick without doing his due diligence. He asked around the community about Nick before confirming he would take him into his home, and the reviews were conclusively negative, with most people labelling Nick as hopeless and bad news. As it turned out, Ronnie, whose own past, big heart, and desire to serve had long since made him a champion of underdogs, saw something in Nick that no one else did—a spark of hope, the potential for transformation. Ronnie later told Nick that the more bad things he heard about Nick, the more he wanted to take a chance and help him. He knew it was possibly Nick's last opportunity, and he knew the power of one more chance.

The first night at Ronnie's house, Nick was antsy, nervous, and wondering if he had made the right decision. In withdrawal and full of doubt, his brain did what addicted brains do: it looked for relief from the pain. He hatched a plan to sneak out and try to get a small amount of dope to help him through the night. With his backpack loaded, Nick stood on the precipice of leaving the last opportunity he might have to save his own life. He knew he risked being expelled yet again, but the obsession was so ingrained that he felt helpless to resist its pull. But something within him halted his steps. Exhausted by it all, with his backpack slung over his shoulder, he paused in the doorway, a heavy sigh escaping from his mouth as his head hung low. "What am I doing?"

Ronnie believed something was possible for him when everyone else gave up. Nick had told healthcare workers not to give up on him only months before. If he left, he was giving up on himself. He knew he had a choice to make.

The moment of truth was here.

Nick whispered to himself, "What if I stayed, and what if I prayed?"

These questions became the catalysts for Nick's transformation. He chose to stay. He chose to pray. The following day, he confided in Ronnie about his near departure.

Ronnie's response was enthusiastic, generous, and kind. "This is fantastic news. By telling me, you've given me the chance to help you." Nick's journey toward recovery began with a question that led to a decision that changed everything. His first weeks in recovery were challenging, and there were tough moments for Nick and the people who took a chance on him, but they were on to something with their approach, one that hadn't been tried in the twenty or so previous treatment centres. Unfailingly, they asked the question, *"What does it look like to love him?"*

It turns out that love looks good on my son.

www.pamrader.com

Catalyst of Conscience

by Luke Wiltshire

I reach under my car seat and bring out my 9mm pistol. I pull the slide back a quarter-inch to make sure a round is in the chamber, release it with a click, and it is locked and loaded. I eject the magazine to make sure there are no malfunctions, slam the slide back into place, and then rest it on my lap. I am thinking about the new hollow-point bullets I purchased earlier this week.

I look down at my pistol—so much a part of me, it's like an extension of my arm. I've shot it thousands of times. So much so that a callus formed on my trigger finger. Tonight, this one last time—I lift it. It feels like the hundred-pound dumbbells from the gym. I put the barrel to my right temple, and without a second thought or inclination, I pull the trigger. Click.

It misfires.

Before I can even register what just happened, I fling the door open and puke. I rip off my balaclava and throw it in the back seat. Sweat cascades down my face, and I swear I can hear my heart booming in my chest. I look at the weapon with confusion. I rack the slide, and the round in the chamber ejects; I catch it, just as I had practised hundreds, if not thousands, of times. I look at the primer, and there is a dimple in it. I projectile vomit out the open driver's side door again, and suddenly my world dims. My chest tightens, and a vice grip squeezes the air from my lungs. Each breath is a struggle, a desperate gasp for oxygen that never fills the void. My heart pounds against my ribs like a frantic drummer in a macabre symphony. It's a rhythm that echoes in my ears, drowning out the world around me.

A cold sweat breaks out across my skin, a chilling contrast to the inferno raging within. My hands tremble uncontrollably, each finger a jittery marionette with a mind of its own. My vision blurs; the edges of the world dissolve into a dizzying kaleidoscope.

Fear, raw and primal, floods my senses; a suffocating wave threatens to pull me under. Thoughts race through my mind—a chaotic whirlwind of anxieties and worst-case scenarios. I try to grasp onto something, anything, to anchor myself in reality. The current is too strong.

I feel utterly alone, trapped in a prison of my own making. My stomach empties of all but bile, and disappointment rushes in, and I almost scream to some unknown deity, "Now is the time you intervene?!" The world outside becomes a distant echo, muffled and distorted. It's as if I'm watching myself from afar, a terrified spectator in a horror film.

The attack peaks—a crescendo of terror that leaves me trembling and exhausted. Gradually, the storm subsides, heaving me up on the shores of reality, battered and bruised.

I take a shaky breath; the air finally reaches my lungs. The world slowly comes back into focus; the colours are muted and dull. I'm left with a lingering sense of dread; my mind won't stop. I have sacrificed my morals, values, and ethics and destroyed my relationships, people's lives, and most importantly, my own family. The recovery counsellor's recent warning haunted me. "You're about to cross a line. You won't know when you'll cross it. You will lose all morality and ethics and become a true psychopath with no shred of your former self remaining. Once crossed, you won't be able to return."

His words reverberated through my brain as the boss gave me the kill order for tonight's deadbeat. A suspected informant. I've had enough of taking their fucking orders.

Tears continue to flood down my face as I think of my mom. All of her sleepless nights. She cries at the thought of not knowing where I am or if I am even alive. I've shattered her heart and soul. The suffering she goes through every second of every day drives shame like a stake into my aching chest. I have never felt this level of shame before—a nagging, dark entity that lurks within, threatening to take over.

I hate myself vehemently, so much so that I did not know or plan to place the barrel at my temple. The shock of the misfire vibrating through me. Why?

I am not sure how long I wept. When my breath returns to normal, I manage to pull myself together. I close my door, grab the rear-view mirror, and turn it toward my face. I don't recognize the monster looking back at me. I flick on the interior light and start the car again. My eyes are black. Dead eyes, most call them. A look that strikes fear in even the most hardened men. This animal, looking back at me, is not the kid who grew up in a small town with loving parents and amazing friends. It bears no resemblance to that sensitive child who had his innocence taken away from him at eight years old by predators far worse than I had become. The reality of who I am sets in at that moment. A cowardly, weak, immoral shell of a man.

From the time of my abuse at the hands of two coaches the summer I was eight years old, something broke inside me. It was like my soul had been fractured, and a crucial part of what made me human leaked from an internal wound and never returned.

Yet, I miss my parents. I miss my dog. I feel a hollowness that only people who experience tremendous suffering know. A soulless void, a black hole of darkness that swallows all that is good; only emptiness returns.

Later that night, a child appears and changes everything for me.

~

In limbo, after that misfire, loading and unloading the gun, I took note of the black night. I sat, looking out at the street ahead. Pulling in a deep breath, I turned the ignition off. All was eerily silent and unusually dark that frigid December night. Dressed in my usual attire, all black: winter jacket, balaclava rolled up toque style and ready to be rolled down to cover my face at any time, tactical gloves embedded with powdered lead, cargo pants, and waterproof assault boots. I always made sure to dress warm on nights like that because I never knew if I might have to chase a buyer or escape a threat. Being on foot for an extended period of time came with all sorts of risks. My life was unpredictable.

The streetlight of the gas station, a half-block ahead on my left, flickered. The cold was comforting. There was and still is something primal about winter that tests my resilience; I respected it. I checked my mirrors and didn't see any people around. I took a deep breath and looked at my watch; it read 9:30 p.m. "Where is this fucking guy?" I ask nobody in particular. My mind drifted.

During my life, I have gained skills that are essential to surviving the streets. Hyper-vigilance, sensory sensitivity, fine-tuned attention to detail, and an unwavering trust in my intuition. Of all my skills, compartmentalization is my crux. It allowed me to do the horrible things I did and was about to do. Addiction to mind-altering substances added to my ability to live in the shadows. I knew no other way forward.

I leaned my seat back and adjusted my mirrors to maintain my view over the dash. I couldn't get enough air sitting straight up. I had to compose myself. I remembered the downers I hid in my coat. I grabbed two of them from my inner pocket and quickly crushed them for consumption. I prepared two one-inch lines of powder on the CD case reserved for this activity. Placed a straw to my nose, I leaned down and snorted both lines at once. A real pro.

The drug hit me like a speed train—within seconds, I felt a warmth spread through my body—a comforting sensation, like a warm blanket enveloping me and soothing my nerves.

As the warmth continued to spread, my muscles relaxed, and I felt a sense of calm wash over me. The anxiety that had been so overwhelming just moments prior became a distant memory, replaced by a gentle numbness.

My breath slowed and deepened, as if my body was finally able to take a full breath without the constant reminder of what I'd become. My thoughts halted; the world around me moved in slow motion. I felt a sense of detachment, as if I were floating above my body, observing the scene from a distance. The worries and fears that had been plaguing me faded away, replaced by a sense of tranquility. I felt a heaviness in my eyelids, and my body grew heavy as if gravity had increased its pull on me.

That first burst of tranquility wasn't mine for long. I experienced a wave of dizziness and a sense of disorientation. My thoughts became jumbled. I struggled to focus on the environment around me. The car spun. I closed my eyes to steady myself. I remember those moments feeling suspended in the veil between life and death. Visions, hallucinations—I couldn't tell what was reality or what might show up in my future if I couldn't escape this life. Macabre visions burned and threatened behind my closed eyelids that were just too heavy to open. I couldn't escape my own mind.

I looked down on a burnt, lifeless body at my feet—a corpse. Was it mine? It had a pungent, acrid smell, almost metallic, with hints of sulphur and ammonia—a heavy, lingering odour that clung to my nose and throat. The smell of charred bone was a dry, ashy smell, somewhat similar to burnt wood but with a more organic, mineral-like undertone. The singed hair was somewhat sweet but also nauseating, like burning plastic. The smouldering coals and remains assaulted all my senses. This shadow of a person was once someone who hurt people.

Time flashed forward and backward. Simultaneously, I pulled the trigger over and over until the gun clicked. I ejected the magazine, and heard the whip-cracking of the bullets that flew around me. I could feel the wind and side-draft from the rounds that danced past me. I loaded another magazine and looked up to see nobody there.

Time slowed down as I pushed the steel of my seven-inch fixed blade knife between his 3rd and 6th ribs directly into his heart. It was over as fast as it started. As his body weight fell, the knife slid out, and with it, a slop sound. Within seconds, there were pints of blood covering the floor. That metallic smell overwhelmed my nostrils, but I was used to it.

Stuck in a deep, drug-induced bad trip, not the release I sought, my head rested against the cold glass of the car window. The world around me was a hazy blur, a distorted dreamscape that felt both familiar and foreign. I was lost in the abyss of my own mind; the tendrils of a drug-induced coma wrapped around me like a straitjacket, the nightmares blurred and distorted with no relief.

~

Until a loud, insistent banging on the passenger door jolted me awake. My heart raced as I struggled to make sense of the noise, my mind still clouded by the remnants of the narcotic. For a moment, I thought it was the cops, their harsh voices, and flashing lights invading my fragile sanctuary.

But as I blinked to focus my eyes and peered through the fogged-up window, I saw and recognized the face. The man I waited to meet, the suspected rat wasn't alone. He had a child with him, a small, innocent, trembling figure standing beside him in the cold. The realization hit me like a punch to the gut. I felt a wave of shame and guilt wash over me, a sickening feeling that twisted my insides and then the first waves of anger. "You fucking brought your kid here… to this… to buy drugs?"

The child, helpless, looked down at the street. I couldn't say if I saw myself in that child then, but I remember feeling the adrenaline rush of rage.

I fumbled with the door handle, and my hands shook as I opened it. The cold air rushed in, a sharp contrast to the shelter of the car. I stepped out, my legs unsteady beneath me, and faced the man and his child.

"Hey," I glared, making a nodding motion with my head toward the child, silently getting my point across. "Seriously…?" He shrugged and lowered his head, still not saying a word.

I looked at the child. My whole persona, which I had honed for years, completely collapsed, like a landslide, at the sight of those innocent eyes that looked up at me. I looked back at the man, then at the child again, and motioned towards the car, "Put the kid in the back seat where it's warm." I could feel my gun in my waistband, and I remember thinking nothing in the car could hurt the child because I had the downers in my coat, the cocaine was in the trunk, and along with my gun, all my weapons were on me.

The man's face was a mask of disappointment and anger, and his eyes were filled with a mixture of sadness and frustration. He didn't say a word. He knew better. I watched as he put the child in the back seat. I waited until he closed the door and turned to face me. "Did you expect me to take this child as payment?"

With pinpoint precision, I punched him directly in the nose—it exploded in a mist of red, and his head whipped back; he fell to the ground holding his face, spitting out two teeth. I didn't want to neutralize him or hurt him badly; I simply wanted him to know he fucked up. He got the point. I could see the specks of blood all over my car and the pavement around where his head was hunched over.

"Get up." I pulled him to his feet. He didn't make a noise. I had seen that look a thousand times. No amount of punishment could compare to the shame he felt at that moment. It trumped everything, awakening in him the safety of his own child as paramount.

I threw a rag at him as I opened the passenger door. "Put that on your face, and don't get any blood in my car." I slid behind the wheel and noticed the child had pulled two of my old Mexican blankets over his entire body. I could only see a lump under the blankets and heard a light, breathing sound emanating from the heap. I looked over at the man sitting in my passenger seat. He did not look at me; he was busy stopping the blood coming from his face with the old rag. Usually, I would have given this man his drugs, and he would have given me money, and we would have parted ways. Not tonight. He had brought a child with him to purchase illicit drugs from a psychopathic, drug-addicted monster—me. He was a suspected rat. I had orders, but that night, nothing was normal. I wasn't following procedure anymore.

We sat in silence for what seemed like an eternity. I could hear the man wiping blood from his nose. I felt my anger dissipate, and listened to the child sleeping; he was safe. For the child, I felt empathy—for the first time in as long as I could remember. It was almost indescribable. A strange calmness enveloped me as a plan took hold.

"Okay, John, I need you to listen to me. Look at me!" I barked. He snapped his head around to face me. Surprisingly, the child stayed asleep. I whispered, "I will no longer be selling to you, and neither will any of my guys." He tried to speak, and I snapped a quick backhand that connected directly with his nose again. He whimpered in pain. "Do you have any money to buy food for your son?" I asked. I was dead serious, and he knew it.

"No," he admitted.

I had no idea how he planned to buy his drugs that night, not that it mattered. None of it mattered to me anymore in the presence of that child. I wasn't going to pull the trigger. Instead, I reached into my pocket and pulled out $3000. I handed him the cash. I have never forgotten the look in his eyes: confusion, gratitude, fear, and anger wrapped into one puffy, blood-soaked face. I flipped my thumb toward the backseat and continued my self-righteous monologue. "Use that money to buy food and Christmas presents for your son. Now, you really need to hear what I'm telling you." I looked at him, and he nodded vigorously, still holding the rag under his now grotesque, swollen nose. "If I hear from anyone that you use that money to buy anything other than what I said, I will fucking bury you where I find you." My eyes locked on him; he was visibly shaking. He mumbled something that I couldn't understand. "All I need from you is a nod."

He nodded. I looked back. The kid was still sound asleep.

As we drove, the only sounds were the car's heater humming and John silently weeping, his face turned toward the passenger window, away from my gaze. My entire life flashed before me in an instant. *Am I having a spiritual experience?* The only other time I felt something like that was on a dark night in a sprawling city over a decade ago. I was shooting at a man who was also trying to kill me. We were fifteen feet apart, firing as fast as we could while moving laterally. I heard the bullets whipping by me as I aimed for his centre mass. He was so close that I could see the whites of his eyes. After the smoke had settled and the brass had finished clanging on the street, we stood facing each other, staring directly into each other's souls. We both nodded, then turned and walked away. I still have nightmares where every bullet strikes me. For most of my life, I felt destined to die gloriously in battle, like a Spartan.

I pulled up to John's apartment complex and parked the car. We sat in silence for an eternity. John looked over at me; his nose had stopped bleeding. I stared and nodded for him to get out. He did. He opened the back door, his child woke up, and I remember his soft, sleepy voice, "I'm hungry, Daddy." John scooped his son out of the back seat and closed the door. He glanced at me as he carried his son toward the apartment. I intentionally watched until he disappeared around the corner.

As I sat in the darkness, the weight of my actions and the life I led crushed me. As a criminal and an addict, I felt trapped. The realization and the day-to-day life hurled me about like a hurricane. I remember thinking, I can't keep doing this... That was the first moment in my life where I felt the need to do what was right.

It was a spark in the void, a tiny flicker of hope.

John wasn't supposed to leave my car alive that night in December. Had my pistol not misfired, I'd be dead, and somebody else would have carried out the kill order.

But by some divine intervention, it was me meeting him, and had he not brought his child with him, three things would have happened: John would be gone, that child would be fatherless, and I would have lost my last shred of humanity, possibly ending up in prison. The presence of that innocent child saved us both in more ways than one. That child presented a line I refused to cross.

I wiped my final tears, my resolve hardening. That night was the beginning of my road to redemption. The path ahead would be fraught with challenges, but I felt a glimmer of purpose for the first time. *"If I can feel this way for this kid, I can feel this way for myself."* I put the car in gear, my hands still shaking, but a new determination thrummed through my heart.

Driving through that night, I made a silent promise to myself and to that child: I will change. I will fight this battle within me and reclaim my soul from the darkness that has consumed it for so long. This is my chance to do what's right, to make amends, and to find a way back to the person I once was, or at least to become someone better.

As I pulled into my driveway, the first light of dawn began to break on the horizon. Though the journey was far from done, I had reclaimed a shadow of my former self and a tiny shred of morality by refusing to carry out the orders. Punished for my non-compliance and other mini rebellions that followed, I was kidnapped and tortured for three days. My captors broke both my legs and arms. I survived even though they left me to die up a deserted logging road in winter. I crawled seven kilometres in boxing shorts and a t-shirt. I landed in jail and barely survived a violent stabbing by an inmate. It was then that my steps on my spiritual awakening journey coalesced. My desire to use drugs and alcohol abruptly vanished. I can't explain it in any other way. From the misfire to the stabbing, I had been spared. For what?

Released from jail, rising above the despair of my previous life, a profound transformation was ignited. Through relentless perseverance, recovery, and education, I forged a new purpose in service to others. That last near death marked the onset of my commitment to aiding others in their own quests for healing. Through the eyes of that child, I found my first step on the long, arduous road to true redemption. Motivated by a deep-seated desire to make a lasting impact, I returned to school and completed the Addictions and Social Service Worker program. Currently, I serve as a peer support specialist in BC's Interior Health, extending crucial support to marginalized individuals grappling with addiction and mental health challenges. Proving that no matter how bad life gets, healing and recovery are possible.

Today, with 10 years of recovery, I stand as a beacon of hope and resilience, having successfully battled my personal demons. I've honed my skills as a personal development mentor, recovery expert, and addiction consultant. I've guided countless individuals through their darkest times, helping them reclaim their lives and reconnect with their loved ones. Through my work, I've reunited families, facilitated healing in group therapy, and taught the power of ownership and responsibility. Each success story is a testament to the strength of the human spirit and the transformative power of truth and compassion. The journey continues, and with every step, I am reminded of the profound impact we can have on one another's lives. This is my mission, my purpose, and I embrace it with an open heart and unwavering determination. For John, for that child, for myself, and most importantly, for all the ones who need a way out of the darkness.

www.thelukewiltshire.com

The Trauma Landscape

by Danna Bushell

Where my son's feet bulged through his tattered socks and soleless shoes, they were bloodied, blistered, and raw. As I cleaned and bandaged his wounds, I was pained and shocked at the sight, but I also wondered, by this simple act of care, was I enabling my son? Was I interfering with him "hitting bottom?" Months after I left him homeless on the street at an addiction professional's prompting, I thought to myself, *he must be close to "hitting bottom" by now*. This is perhaps the starkest memory I have of those early days of my son's substance use disorder (SUD), when I was desperate to help my son and willing even to abandon him to some elusive bottom if that's what the "experts" said would help.

When I became aware of my son's struggle with SUD, I felt as if I'd been suddenly dropped into an abyss. Effective inpatient treatment was impossible to find. When he was ready to enter treatment, invariably, a bed was not available. When I would finally receive a call that a bed was available, he would already be lost to the streets. When I was able to get my son into treatment, four or five days into an inpatient stay, I'd receive a call that he had left rehab, had overslept and missed group therapy, or in some other way was demonstrating that he "wasn't ready" for treatment. My son told me numerous times that the group counselling and 12-step meetings in rehab did nothing to help him.

I concurred with the counsellors and resigned myself, as they did, that my son was just not "ready" for recovery. Never was it mentioned to me that the accepted medical standard of care for my son's condition is medication for opioid use disorder (MOUD), chiefly methadone or buprenorphine. The narrative from rehab centres was always that my son had failed treatment, never that the treatment provided was failing my son because it did not meet the accepted standard of care for opioid use disorder (OUD). Never once did a rehab suggest or provide these long-researched and validated medications, which are widely regarded by institutions such as the World Health Organization, the Canadian Medical Association, the American Society of Addiction Medicine, and the American Medical Association as the first-line, best practice standard of care for OUD.

Instead, when turning to mutual aid groups and rehab professionals, they'd instruct me that the most helpful thing I could do for my son was "detach," "let go and let God," and wait for my son to "hit bottom." When my natural parental instincts would revolt at these directives and I would dare to verbalize my ambivalence about abandoning my son, they'd warn me of the perils of becoming "codependent" or "enabling" and encourage me to quiz myself as to whether I was "loving my child," or "loving my child to death."

It is in similar contexts to what I experienced that many parents of children with substance use issues find themselves engulfed in shame and internalized stigma. On the one hand, the treatment and mutual aid industries give us the message that following our parental instincts to protect and help our children is somehow pathological. On the other hand, the larger society often sends the message that we somehow did not do enough to prevent our children from falling into SUD in the first place.

Isolation often ensues as parents struggle to make healthy decisions in relationships with their children while also suffering in silence and shame, unable to turn in a genuine and heart-centred way to either the recovery community or the community at large. Parents are marginalized by *external stigma* from a society that moralizes and mischaracterizes problematic substance use. We are simultaneously torn by an *internalized stigma* that leaves us paralyzed in the face of how to effectively address our children's SUD.

Parents are struggling with the most terrifying and traumatic events of our lifetimes—and we do so alone—as we witness our children repeatedly skirt death and tumble further into addiction. Chronically witnessing and responding to the emergencies and negative repercussions of our children's problematic substance use in the context of such limited support can impart trauma to family members, which impacts us for years to come.

Early in my son's struggle with SUD, he repeatedly suffered near-fatal heroin overdoses. The initiation of a long trail of trauma for the entire family began for me with a frantic call from my former husband as he raced to where paramedics were resuscitating our son from his first overdose. He only survived because his girlfriend, too afraid to dial 911, called my former husband, who in turn called emergency services. The paramedics were almost too late.

My heart still races and snags raw in my throat when I remember the night my son overdosed on a park bench and was only discovered as paramedics responded to another witnessed overdose nearby. My ears still recoil as they echo the panic from his frantic cries when he called me from the emergency room, confused as to why his clothing was in shreds and dangling from his skin—the vestige of the heroic efforts enacted by emergency workers trying to gain intravenous access to reverse yet another of the accidental overdoses my son miraculously survived. He wore the hospital bracelet from that night until it disintegrated from his wrist, but even that frightful reminder of his skirt with death was insufficient to deter him from returning to heroin use.

There were times when my son's father and I would not hear from our son for many weeks. We would divide the dreaded tasks in the hope of finding him. I would call the area hospitals. My ex would call the morgues. With no answers, desperation and wild mother instinct would abduct my better judgment. I would find myself wandering the streets I suspected he frequented, showing his photo to anyone I came across who appeared to me to be just as estranged from one's mother as my son—torn, weathered backpacks, and downward gazes being telltale signs.

Many will call me foolish or reckless, or both. Perhaps I am reckless at times, yet my most reckless moments occasionally impart the greatest wisdom. I can say assuredly that the humanity, compassion, and grace I witnessed in the eyes that most of us avoid—those of the unhoused and addicted that we'd prefer to keep invisible—far surpasses any kindness, gratitude, or humility I've witnessed from those in glass high-rises, tech-bro hangouts, or the evangelical mega-churches of my youth.

These folks lived—with immediacy—the fact that this day and the next are not a given. They inhabited impermanence so ubiquitous and raw that their natural response to another's pain and worry was compassion devoid of belittling stigma.

As I shared my son's photo along with my worry and fear, I was met with understanding and empathy as folks on the street shared their own stories of missing loved ones and friends lost to an overdose. By opening myself to those I once dismissed and marginalized and witnessing their struggles firsthand, I experienced a paradigm shift from stigma and avoidance to compassion and understanding. Perhaps we stigmatize, avert our eyes, and marginalize traumatized people because it is easier to blame them for their pain than bear witness.

And yet, parents of children with addiction do not so easily make that choice. We are live witnesses as our children struggle and suffer, often to devastating ends. I was horribly torn between my desire to help my son and the intolerable pain of watching him almost die when, after a particularly traumatic overdose experience, I asked him not to call me the next time he overdosed. For a time, I could no longer watch him put his life in such jeopardy. Some of us simply reach a point beyond which we can bear, and we must turn away. Regardless of how we react outwardly to the experience of watching our children fall prey to SUD, I'd venture to say that most parents suffer our own psychic injuries from what we've witnessed and battled against. Even after he achieved several years of recovery, I still struggled (and still struggle to this day) with lingering trauma born from my son's early struggles with SUD.

Compounded Trauma

I slouched over my laptop and pounded the keys in a tantrum as I logged in to yet another telehealth appointment with my mental health care provider. This time, would she at least increase my dose or add on a second antidepressant so maybe I could get some relief? After a quick hello, she asked about my symptoms. "I can't move. I suppose my mood has improved some in the last few months, but the antidepressant isn't working as well as it was. I am just stuck. There is so much I need to be doing, but I sit, frozen, unable to accomplish a thing."

A few weeks prior, I had failed two classes for non-participation and been kicked out of the university program I was attending to further my nursing career. In my twenties, I had pushed hard and was an accomplished student, often at the top of my class in nursing school. What was wrong with me now? I'd always succeeded at anything I put my mind to. Why did I now feel so overwhelmed, anxious, and unable to push through?

"Your symptoms sound consistent with c-PTSD. Do you have a history of trauma?"

"Doc, you mean chronic PTSD? If so, I probably do. I mean, the last few years have been non-stop trauma, watching my son struggle with substance use disorder." After all, the worst of my collapse into depression and immobility had begun after my son achieved many months of recovery, at which point I had some distance from being on constant high alert for his next overdose or worse.

"*Complex*, not chronic PTSD. However, it is true that complex PTSD is caused by prolonged trauma, including ongoing emotional, physical, or sexual abuse, which can begin at any age."

My gut jarred with recognition, and shame flooded my face. I could not remember a day of my childhood that was free from a barrage of humiliation and insults. The abuse was perpetual and had embedded itself in my psyche, deeply affecting my view of myself and how I moved in the world. Hearing her description of c-PTSD, it became clear to me that my early trauma was related to the depression I had struggled with to one degree or another as far back as I could remember.

Still, I had never felt this empty and exhausted in my earlier struggles with depression. In a moment of realization, I pondered, *Can it be that I am struggling with c-PTSD from both my childhood and these recent years of witnessing my son's struggle with SUD?*

How would I get past this? Was there any effective help? My thoughts trailed off into worries for my son. I swallowed hard, recalling how my upbringing had left me ill-equipped for motherhood.

The intergenerational impact of trauma
Due to the trauma I suffered in childhood, I developed poor relational skills, bouts of depression, and anxious, insecure attachments in adult relationships. These factors created a chaotic dynamic in my life, which left me unable to provide a child with the nurturance needed for a healthy

upbringing, let alone discern the warning signs as serious problems began to develop in my son's life.

In Al-Anon, a mutual aid group for friends and families of people with addiction, there is a saying referred to as "The Three Cs: I didn't cause it. I can't control it, and I can't cure it." I only subscribe to this slogan on its margins. While I know I did not cause my son's SUD, I no doubt contributed to its development. And while I agree that I cannot control or cure it, I do believe that parents and family members can have a much greater influence on their loved ones' healing and recovery than many Al-Anon groups would have people believe.

I understand that there is a plethora of factors that lead a person to develop a substance use disorder and that various theories of addiction abound. I personally view the development of addiction as a dreaded perfect storm. The bio-psycho-social model of addiction describes the phenomenon well, which posits that no one factor causes addiction but that multiple factors meet, which cause a person to be particularly susceptible to SUD. Variables such as the substance consumed and the amount, a person's biological, genetic, and psychological traits, as well as the socio-cultural conditions they are surrounded by, all contribute to a person's risk of developing a SUD. While I know I am not single-handedly responsible for his addiction, my relationship with my son, from his earliest years onward, was, at the very least, a factor that impacted its development.

I still struggle with guilt and regret. I often wonder if I had only been more present and invested in my son's life, rather than rummaging through the fog of my own anguish during his early years, might I have been able to help him avoid some of the pain he later suffered? I imagine many people, even those from the most well-adjusted families, also wonder what they could have done differently when they learned of a loved one's addiction.

I should have done more early on to prioritize my son and his wellbeing, and my own upbringing left me ill-equipped to do so. I am not blaming the person who abused me. I am stating the facts and describing what happened. I take responsibility for my actions. And also, I allow myself the same grace I've afforded the person who traumatized me at a young age. On my more resilient days, I have the compassion to know deeply that we all do the best we can with what we have at any given time.

Still, my voice shakes when I admit to having been a "not good enough" mother at times. Too often, I believe, we struggle in our society to decouple causation from blame, shame, and stigma. Yet, only by breathing light into dark corners, unearthing, and exposing these shameful secrets can we heal and prevent further trauma. Trauma does not occur in a vacuum, and so I trust I am not alone. I know there must be other mothers out there like me, struggling to heal from past injuries, kicking themselves for their parenting foibles or failures, all the while having this trauma compounded as they witness their children's perilous struggles with addiction.

I imagine there are many other parents sitting in quiet corners grappling with a new c-PTSD diagnosis or perhaps a misdiagnosis with depression or borderline personality disorder, for which c-PTSD is sometimes mistaken. As we do all we can to seek healing for our children, we must remember that we, as parents, are worthy and deserving of safety and healing, too.

Recovering from c-PTSD
The childhood abuse I suffered has been a central theme throughout the many years of therapy I've attended for the treatment of depression and relational issues. While I have learned a great deal and made many positive changes in my life through the years, my inner critic still has an outsized influence on my life, leaving me immobilized at times and negatively affecting my relationships. For all the healing I've accomplished, I sense there is a deep, young core of wounding that talk therapy alone has failed to access. For as much progress as I've made in learning healthy boundaries and regulating my emotions, my system was nonetheless unguarded and unprepared for the trauma I would endure with my son's struggles with SUD.

Learning about c-PTSD has given me new insight into my struggles with my early and more recent trauma and new avenues of healing and recovery to explore. Complex PTSD may present with the symptoms common to PTSD, such as hyper-arousal, nightmares, flashbacks, and severe anxiety. However, people with c-PTSD may also experience feelings of shame and worthlessness, difficulty controlling emotions, trouble feeling connected with others, and problems maintaining relationships with partners and friends.

In addition to its impact on mental health, the chronic stress of conditions such as c-PTSD can also lead to physical illness, and parents may find themselves diagnosed with diabetes, hypertension, or other stress-related illnesses secondary to the trauma they've survived. The wider societal health impact of chronic diseases developed secondary to trauma is untold, especially amid a prolonged opioid overdose epidemic. I suspect the diabetes I developed during my son's struggles was at least in part hastened by chronic stress and trauma, and I know many other parents of children with SUD who've been similarly diagnosed with stress-related illnesses.

In learning more about the impact of trauma, I discovered that the symptoms I've experienced over many years, which have been diagnosed for decades as major depressive disorder, are much more aligned with the symptoms of c-PTSD. I am sure the two have co-existed at various points in my life, but rather than being an additional burden, I find the diagnosis of c-PTSD brings me hope, as there are burgeoning new models and therapies for understanding and treating trauma beyond conventional talk therapy.

Traditional methods of therapy apply what many therapists and researchers refer to as a top-down approach, which utilizes the area of the brain responsible for consciousness and thought processes to help clients alter how they respond to symptoms of depression, PTSD, and a variety of troubling mental health issues. Other recently discovered and renewed theories posit that trauma is experienced in deeper, more primitive areas of the brain and, when not worked through or released, can lead to a disruption of our natural, neurologically driven fight-flight-freeze-fawn responses. In a bottom-up approach, somatic therapies aim to employ the deeper areas of the brain to gently release frozen trauma responses by engaging the client's awareness of bodily sensations and movements.

Early research into somatic therapies is promising, showing improvement in emotional and physical symptoms for people with PTSD, although larger studies are needed to develop a strong evidence base. What is clear anecdotally, however, is that, as helpful and necessary as talk therapy is, many people "hit a wall" as they process trauma in traditional therapy. They find, as I do, that there are aspects of trauma that cannot be accessed or healed by cognitive means alone.

There are many types of somatic therapy, from eye movement desensitization and reprocessing (EMDR) to somatic experiencing, brainspotting, and trauma-informed yoga. Some consider various forms of meditation to contain a somatic element as well, and I agree. Adopting a daily meditation practice has been transformative for me in many regards. Utilizing both single-pointed breathing meditation and analytical meditation has helped me immensely to become more aware of my self-defeating and self-shaming thoughts and to treat myself and others with greater compassion and acceptance.

Healing Intergenerational Wounds
For all the shame I carry regarding the ways I traumatized my son, I am at once relieved and concerned regarding the recent research on intergenerational trauma. There is evidence that trauma-related genetic changes can be passed down—pre-conceptually—for at least two generations.

As Rachel Yehuda, professor of psychiatry and neuroscience at Mount Sinai School of Medicine, so eloquently demonstrates in an article for Scientific American, studies with the children of Holocaust survivors, Vietnam veterans, and mice show that epigenetic changes—changes in how genes turn on and off and produce proteins—can be handed down to multiple generations and cause offspring to be more sensitive to traumatic events. This may be a biological adaptation to help offspring be better prepared for dangerous situations. However, it may also cause the children of parents who suffered from PTSD to be more susceptible to similar symptoms themselves. Could the field of epigenetics hold answers to how intergenerational trauma is passed down beyond the relational dynamics between parent and child?

Though more research is needed to confirm the early science, the building consensus is that intergenerational trauma is influenced by both nurture and nature. Could it be that how I processed my early childhood abuse was in part influenced by my parents' and even my grandparents' epigenetic alterations? And might I have passed down these same genetic markers of trauma to my son? If it is true that trauma is trapped in the body and even passed down from generation to generation, are families such as mine doomed to ongoing intergenerational legacies of such wounding?

Yehuda brings us hope as she shares that in studies of the intergenerational epigenetics of trauma with mice, the offspring mice were able to be conditioned out of their trauma responses and did not pass down the same epigenetic alterations they inherited from their parents. My hope is that, by utilizing various therapies and practices that help us release stored trauma and build resilience, humans can do the same.

My son has enjoyed many years of sobriety, be it with some brief returns to use. His father and I refuse to see these slips as having plummeted him to ground zero in his recovery. Instead, we encourage him to hold on to the esteem of his overall accomplishments. He knows that he has succeeded in the past and can succeed again, and that even if he continues to use, we will meet him where he is and support him in ways that are helpful to him and safe for us, a methodology known as harm reduction. By employing harm reduction as a family, my son's episodes of returning to use have been briefer and much less devastating than early in his addiction, when we were hyper-focused on avoiding enabling, utilizing tough love, and waiting for some elusive bottom to hit.

Still, my son is resistant to seeking any counselling for the trauma he has surely suffered or even talking with me personally about it. However, he also knows I take accountability for the times my mothering fell short. He knows he has an open invitation to work toward healing past trauma with me at any point if he so chooses. I yearned for many years to establish healing with the person who neglected and abused me as a child, and I have long-faced regrets for that person's unwillingness or inability to engage in such a process. Presently, my son has a different view about the importance of intergenerational healing, and that must be okay. While I feel deep regret for the trauma I passed down, a weight he's not yet ready to address, I must accept that we each travel our own path. For now, I focus on my own healing journey.

I do not view healing as a linear journey, nor do I think it will culminate at some sharp endpoint of "I am healed now" in my lifetime. And perhaps this acceptance is the first sign of healing from trauma: the acceptance that healing is a lifetime process and that I am not worth less or defective as a human being for the wounds I carry. In fact, my willingness to heal and the very wounds themselves impart a certain strength to my life that I would not otherwise possess. The traumatic experiences of my life have cracked open in me a greater awareness, openness, and empathy toward the suffering in our world. They've also led me to a more spiritually nuanced understanding of life; happiness is not an endpoint that we achieve that then remains a static constant in our lives.

The desires that we cling to sharply will eventually and inevitably disappoint us, and in just the same way that we can trust that this too shall pass as we address life's challenges, we can trust that our happiest moments will also fade. So perhaps healing is about learning to roll with the tide of these ebbs and flows, approaching both the joy and pain of life with equanimity.

Perhaps healing is about bringing a harm reduction ethos to our own daily lives, in which we meet life as it comes, day-by-day, soaking in the joyful moments to their fullest and cherishing the memories as we work our way through the painful aspects of life. I do my best to approach my relationship with my son through this balanced lens on life. I hope that by mirroring a more centred and grounded way of living, I might inspire him toward the healing I've enjoyed and minimize the impact of our shared intergenerational trauma.

www.enablehope.net

A Journey of Recovery and Transformation

by Dawn Finn

Isolated in the sanctity of my bedroom, it was 4:33 a.m. when the night teeters on the edge of morning and dreams. A vision flashed before me in that hazy half-sleep—a family photo, eerily missing one beloved face. My son, Andrew, was nowhere to be seen. Dismissing it as a mere trick of the mind, I rolled over, trying to reclaim the comfort of oblivion.

But sleep brought no peace.

By 5:30 a.m., a wrenching sensation in my gut dragged me into complete wakefulness. Compelled by an inexplicable urgency, I ran towards the living room where my cell phone lay. The glowing screen flashed ominously with missed calls—messages from the police department, my son's ex-wife, and Andrew's father. The words they left shattered the silence: "Dawn, Andrew is dead."

The news ran through me, endangering my three decades of hard-won sobriety for a split-second, and then the scream escaped my lips before I could catch it. I called out to my husband, my voice a raw echo in the empty room as the surreal truth set in. My mind reeled back to the dream—the missing figure in the photo, now a haunting premonition.

Oh my God, his son, (my grandson), the thought crashed into me with the next wave of grief. In the stillness of early morning, surrounded by the remnants of my broken sleep, the magnitude of my loss began to sink in. My story, marked by triumphs over personal demons and the journey of recovery, had turned a devastating new page.

Why did this happen? How did this happen? This isn't the life I imagined. I always believed things would turn out differently. He was going to be by my side in running this non-profit. Now, I'm left wondering how to move forward with my own story, dealing with the pain of missing my son, Andrew, and feeling selfish for my grief. What about his siblings and his child? What kind of life will they lead now?

What am I doing alive? What does sobriety even mean when this emotional whiplash looms and threatens me with the lure of escape? Escaping the pain, the grief, the lost dreams...

A week before, I had joined a group called *Thinking into Results*, led by my coach, Tara Pilling, with Diamond Mind Consulting. When the tragedy struck, she gave me the choice: take some time off or lean in. My heart and gut screamed for me to lean in, even though I wasn't sure what it meant. I chose to stay; I felt that was where I needed to be—to learn and to understand. Now, I had to navigate this new reality, where every step forward was weighted with the memory of loss.

With thirty years of sobriety behind me, did I have the tools to fight through this new darkness threatening to overwhelm me? Where would I find the light now when I could never hug him again? Andrew and I would not be running the nonprofit together. We had talked about leaving a legacy of change and how, at any moment, from a year to thirty years of addiction, people can escape the loop of substance use disorder and transform. Not only do I grieve the loss of my oldest son, but I also grieve the loss of my dreams and then berate myself for being selfish. What about Andrew's dreams, my other children, and my grandson?

According to Adverse Childhood Experiences (ACEs) research, I should be in jail or dead. Despite the pain that dominated the early chapters of my life, the story that unfolded is one of remarkable transformation. Relentlessly, I made hope a mandate in my journey from darkness to a life illuminated by unexpected revelations.

My father struggled with addiction, which brought instability and conflict into our home. The violence that ensued from his rage and substance use was unimaginable. I was afraid and never felt good enough. I was unsure of who my real friends were. *Am I safe? Will I have food today?* I look back and realize the instability of my childhood was insurmountable.

I remember a time when we lived in Robbinsdale, Minnesota. At 10, I was the oldest of five children and felt it was my job to protect my siblings. My father and mother were fighting—my mother wanted out of the relationship. Looking back at the years of turmoil she endured, I can see how her choices unfolded.

My father left with another woman a year before we lived in Robbinsdale, and it took months for my mother to start dating again. When she finally did, she met a man who provided the stability and love she needed. He eventually became our stepfather. However, my father returned unexpectedly, demanding to be taken back. One night, we awoke to the sounds of a heated argument. In an effort to comfort my siblings, I assured them I would handle it. My brother and I watched in horror as my father took our mother by the hair and dragged her down the steps into the bathroom that was underneath the stairwell, as he was punching her and calling her names.

I was frozen in confusion. *What can I do?* Intense fear set in while I struggled to understand what was happening in front of me. I remember thinking, *How do I keep my sisters and brother safe?* The truth is, I could not. *The world isn't safe.* I turned to my brother. "Go make sure the others are OK." I ran down the stairs; as fear-ridden as I was, I knew I had to open that bathroom door. My father had a knife at Mom's stomach, threatening to cut the baby out. I started screaming. I believe that had I not screamed, my father, in his enraged state, would have killed my mother and that child. I blanked out until the police arrived at the house. I am told I was the one to call the police, but I have no memory of it. The pain, the fear, the feelings of helplessness that were coursing through every fibre of my being—how does a child of 10 begin to process such memories? It took many years of therapy for this memory to surface and start the healing process.

My father did attend treatment. It was the best thing for him. He was never violent again. He stayed in recovery until his death.

Meanwhile, there were silent battles that no child should have to endure, with trust and safety being breached by those meant to protect me. My maternal grandfather sexually abused me. Moving through these next few years blurred my memory and memories; if I have them, they are a jumble. Both family, friends, aunts, and uncles knew of the addiction; they knew of the violence and the sexual abuse. Not one person I should have been able to count on to protect me did a single thing.

From a young age, I sought escape and solace. I turned to drugs and alcohol, seeking temporary numbness to the chaos around me. The substances provided a fleeting illusion of comfort, masking my pain, fear of others, and unworthiness—all festering beneath the surface. I didn't understand what was going on inside me and certainly didn't know all the ways I thought I was managing—I was merely coping. In those moments, I was a young soul grappling with the weight of unresolved trauma, trying to navigate a boat with no rudder.

Despite these adversities, my story is not defined by them. I had a deep desire, a belief, that there were answers to my unspoken cries, my desperate yearnings for peace, and that some semblance of normalcy, even a life of wholeness, was possible. It was this inner knowing that fuelled the journey of overcoming.

Each moment of adversity in my early years, while deeply challenging, unknowingly steered the paths I would choose later in life. These experiences did not just happen to me—they moulded me, influencing my decisions during my turbulent teenage years and into early adulthood. My teen years were marked by rebellion and confusion, a direct result of the instability and challenges I faced growing up. This period plunged headfirst into poor decisions and misguided actions, leading me further away from the stable and healthy life I longed for.

I struggled to find my place in the world as a young adult. I entered relationships seeking the stability and love I lacked, which led to starting a family at eighteen. Overwhelmed and isolated, I was trying to navigate the tumultuous waters of young parenthood while battling my inner demons. The weight of responsibility was immense. Constantly searching for validation, I faced the harsh realities of life with limited support and guidance. I was ill-prepared to handle it due to my unresolved issues and ongoing struggles with insecurity, desperation, vulnerability, and disillusionment. Every setback deepened feelings of inadequacy and hopelessness. This is the world into which my son Andrew was born:

generational trauma, failed treatments, and brushes with the law. Here I was, trying to protect my son from the same pain I endured while repeating the cycle myself. I was failing miserably. The cycle seemed unbreakable.

As I stood at the crossroads of my life at 28, facing the real possibility of losing my children amidst legal troubles, I knew I had to make a critical decision. The Department of Human and Child Protective Services had already been investigating; the pressure was mounting. Additionally, there was an outstanding warrant for my arrest; I was contemplating turning myself in for selling controlled substances.

It was then that my father, who had maintained his sobriety for many years, delivered an ultimatum: "If you don't get clean and sober, I'm taking your kids."

In a mental whirlwind, I wanted out, but I was afraid of the devil I didn't know—*How do I get started? Do I try AA? It worked for Dad. Should I check into a psych ward—but what would happen to my children?* The answers were beyond my line of sight. I couldn't see them... yet.

There was a glimmer of hope. My neighbour was hanging her wash on the line. She used a phrase I recognized from my father's early sobriety days. Striving to be casual, I shared, "I've been struggling. I need help." Then, tenuously, "Do you attend AA meetings?"

She answered cheerfully. "Yeah, I do. I'll take you."

It was at that moment that I began my fragile journey toward recovery. I delved into this new chapter with a mixture of apprehension and a thirst for a better way to live. Embracing this new path, healing, and understanding transformed my turmoil into a narrative of hope and resilience.

Choosing sobriety was not just a personal decision; it was grasping a lifeline. The support system I found in recovery groups, mentors, and my father, who had walked a similar path, became my anchors. My father's journey to sobriety gave me hope and a sextant to follow. The steps and skills I saw in the people who attended these communities helped me build my map.

That map and that foundation profoundly influenced my relationships with my children. As I worked through my recovery, I was able to be more present and emotionally available for them. The stability and love

I began to foster in our home provided a stark contrast to the chaos and uncertainty they had known.

The strength and hope I found in recovery were not just about overcoming addiction; they prepared me for future challenges, including the devastating loss of Andrew. My journey of sobriety equipped me with the tools to navigate immense grief and pain without resorting to old coping mechanisms. It taught me the importance of facing life's challenges head-on, leaning on my support system, and finding hope even in the most excruciating moments.

When Andrew died, the pain was indescribable. Yet, as I faced the steps necessary to put his body to rest, I felt resilience arise within me that I didn't know I possessed. When waves of grief would crash into me, I also knew how to seek help and support. The principles I learned in recovery—one day at a time, living in the moment, finding gratitude in small things—became my lighthouse, guiding me as I navigated the immense loss of my son.

As the last of my children ventured out to begin their journeys, I had accomplished 18 years of recovery. Andrew had only eleven of those years. He left at seventeen to navigate his journey in the world.

A couple of years later, the shock of an empty nest drove us to brainstorm what was next. My husband mistakenly thought I might want to be closer to my family in Minnesota, in the land of 10,000 lakes, where he could go fishing and pass on his love of outdoor sports to the grandkids. My children stayed behind in Iowa, at least at first.

So did all my support groups and my sobriety—almost. PTSD forced me to become my own friend in these new waters and shores. It was here, amid the quiet snowfalls and serene landscapes, that I encountered Dr. Wayne Dyer's *The Power of Intention*. This book was not just a read; it was a revelation, sparking a profound transformation in how I viewed life and my purpose.

This book reshaped my view of the world, presenting scenarios and insights that were initially hard to embrace. Dr. Dyer discussed that in the spirit realm, we choose the trials, tribulations, and joys of our physical lives here on earth. At first, I rejected this notion—how could I have possibly chosen such a challenging path? Yet, as I took a deeper dive, this perspective sparked a profound awakening.

The realization did not dawn on me immediately; it simmered within me for about a year. When I finally grasped it, I experienced a liberating shift: I was no longer a victim of the undertow. Instead, I understood that my soul had actively chosen these experiences for my growth. Life continued to throw challenges my way, living up to the adage of "life on life's terms."

These were not merely obstacles but lessons steering me towards the truths I sought.

None of us are separate; the ego doesn't rule, and we are all one and here for each other's unfolding. Like the trees in the forest that share resources to heal a damaged sibling, we need to be that for each other. No more blame for me. No more victim mindset. Catching the victim mentality before it took hold was a sport now, and I began to own my thoughts. My worldview changed; a stunning realization emerged: *We are all **truly** connected*. I had found the place I was searching for—I belonged. Intermittently, I sensed something was missing throughout my recovery, particularly at the five-year mark. *There's got to be more to life than this.*

From that moment, the heavens opened, clarity descended, and calm waters enveloped me. This didn't mean my life became perfect, but it marked a major shift in how I viewed my responsibility for my actions, words, and beliefs. I had cleared out the debris of my past, but now I was addressing not just the symptoms of my struggles but the root causes themselves.

As my understanding deepened, so did my application of life's lessons, many of which echoed the timeless adages of the Alcoholics Anonymous program. "Live and let live." "Easy does it." "First things first." "Keep it simple." These phrases were no longer clichés but principles that breathed life into my daily existence. This marked my story's turning point—the moment I realized *I was free to rewrite my narrative*. Embracing this freedom transformed the shackles of victimhood into the wings of autonomy. Here began the true light of freedom, illuminating the spiritual path to rewriting my story on my terms.

This next phase of my life, my spiritual healing, unfolded during a crucial period when my son, Andrew, was deeply entrenched in our generational trauma and his addictions. It was also a time that demanded significant personal growth and reflection on my part. As I navigated my spiritual awakening, Andrew unknowingly mirrored back to me not just challenges but profound life lessons. Our interactions, reflecting the principles I found in recovery groups, became unexpected teachings in the art of living and healing.

Andrew, in his struggles, unintentionally taught me invaluable lessons that aligned with the timeless clichés of recovery communities. "First things first" became a daily mantra, guiding me to prioritize my sobriety and well-being and empowering me to support him more effectively. He taught me to **think**, encouraging a pause for thoughtful reflection before speaking or acting—this was crucial in preventing reactive and often unproductive responses. Perhaps, most importantly, Andrew taught me to **keep it simple**. This lesson reminded me that, in the complexity of addiction and recovery, the simplest approaches often have the most impact.

Reflecting on these interactions, I realize Andrew did not know he was imparting these lessons. Yet, through his actions and the challenges he faced, he became a catalyst for my transformation and a deeper understanding of recovery's core principles. In sharing these experiences, I hope to illuminate how our most trying moments with ourselves and loved ones are the richest sources of personal growth and wisdom.

Andrew and I talked about working together at the nonprofit I spearheaded. I could see him working alongside me. When we talked, he spoke of his deep love for his son, his desire to be close to him, and his desire to be there for him. This vision of the future makes his absence even more sad.

I do talk to Andrew, especially after his death. I have a good understanding of the veil between life and death. We talked about many things. He shared that in my most profound moments of grief, he could see me—but I couldn't hear him. I knew the exact moment when he returned to his light body and began healing from his stay on earth. From that moment on, his soul's healing began. I have found solace in believing and knowing that he is at peace. Andrew died by suicide, a tragic end to his battle with addiction and mental health. The pain of his loss is a heavy burden, but I hold onto the peace he has found—the peace that eluded him in life.

Every day, I grapple with the emotional impact of his absence. The journey of recovery and healing is ongoing, and some days are harder than others. My story is marked by moments of profound grief but also by the relentless pursuit of hope and healing. It is one of survival, resilience, and the unending quest for understanding and peace.

While dealing with the complexities of life, I have discovered that happiness and joy are an inside job. They do not come from external places or things but from within me. This inner knowing, shaped by my experiences, allows me to see the traumas of others and the world and handle them with style, grace, and emotional intelligence. Each day, I find strength in knowing I can build my inner peace, even during the most trying times. This journey through recovery and the strength it has given me are integral parts of my story. They empower me to honour and continue to carry Andrew's memory by helping others who face similar struggles, fostering a legacy of hope, resilience, and change.

As I share these reflections, what I most connect with in my story is the resilience it forged within me—it can be that way for you. This narrative is not just about the hardships but about the bridges built towards hope and recovery, highlighting how knowledge and support transformed my life. Again, the possibility is there for all of us each day that we take another breath. It's a testament to the power of healing and the brighter chapters that can follow even the darkest moments.

If my story touches you, it is an invitation—to celebrate where you are on your journey.

www.linkedin.com/in/dawnfinn

WILDFLOWER:

An Unfinished Love Story

by Anne Theriault

You are about to walk into the middle of a wildflower story dotted with sorrows and joys, scorched ground and miracles, breathtaking moments, and unexpected glimmers of hope. Wildflowers are beautiful non-conformists; they are not broken. They can grow in broken places withstanding the harshest conditions. Wildflowers deserve admiration and freedom.

This is an unfinished love story about addiction and mental health.

Pura Vida
After the minister concludes the service, my daughter takes me aside and mumbles something about cocaine. Sweating profusely, shaking, and crying, she tells me there's a problem. Our family and a proud grandfather have gathered for her brother's wedding. "I need help. I don't know how to stop." A week later, curled up in a ball of physical and emotional pain, she will call an ambulance to her apartment to have her stomach pumped. She calls from the hospital. "I am in a dark place. I don't know what to do." I make my best attempt to salvage the wedding celebration.

Frantically, I begin to search for available private treatment centres. After agonizing weeks of worry and persuasion, she finally consents. The decision, my husband and I believe, needs to be hers. We are certain this type of rehabilitation will certainly put things right. Why has this blindsided us? How could this happen to our daughter? To our close-knit family? Joy drains out of my body, and fear moves in without an invitation.

Numbness soon becomes my constant companion. We take out a significant line of credit. Eventually, there will be five more rounds of private detox and rehab until we are bluntly told that they have nothing left to offer. In our daughter's tenacious strength, she finds a publicly funded treatment program for women. There will be a long list of psychiatric medications, misdiagnoses, additional trauma, and hospitalizations—voluntary and involuntary admissions for depression, relapses, and suicide attempts. There will be several hopeful stretches of sobriety.

Abstinence and recovery attempts over the next few years will offer her wellness and give temporary relief to our family's situation, adding some light to her journey. Sadly, it becomes evident that her drug use is much more complex. Crack, meth, heroin, opioids, and the early days of fentanyl are now in the mix. It will take several more years to be properly diagnosed. A concurrent bi-polar disorder diagnosis, along with substance use disorder, creates the "perfect storm." She will be heavily over-medicated with prescribed powerful psychiatric medications based on a series of incorrect conclusions. The first thing I learn is that the frontal cortex of the brain, the part that makes rational decisions, is not fully developed until a person reaches around age 25. As we will discover much later, this entire situation will have been ten years in the making—deep secrets, multiple traumas, and drug use starting in her teens. Opiates, including fentanyl, were prescribed following a traumatic accident resulting in a broken back at age 16.

We begin to realize we will have no legal access to any health information without her consent. The adult patient decides who receives that privilege. We desperately strive to stay connected to our young, unstable daughter, scrambling to access limited mental health resources and attempting to create stability for the situation. She wants full control of what we know about her health and finances and to be respected as an adult making her own choices and decisions. We make significant efforts to respect her right to privacy to empower her. In our best effort to maintain safe housing regardless of the financial or emotional cost, we take unusual risks: buy a second property, change jobs, and even move provinces. Running in every direction trying to extinguish the threatening fires of self-destruction, our thoughts become catastrophic and guilt-ridden. "We don't know what to do" becomes our response to everything. The power of addiction and mental illness has its claws around our family.

Our beautiful, free-spirited Wildflower is just 24 years old.

> *Trying to write is like lifting cement. Few words adequately express how life feels through all this. It's as if I am behind a locked door. I cannot see what is happening on the other side. I keep looking for bits of gold glitter, for hope in something, even if it's small. My hands are feeling around in the dark, searching for answers, reasons, cures, even for God. "Fix this now!"*
>
> *June 2016 – Anne's journal*

We rationalize about the drug use. Each time she enters detox and treatment, we cautiously exhale and try to stay hopeful. This time. This time.

Just when we think it cannot get worse, we are shocked again.

Navigating these unexplored systems of care, which shut us out with privacy rules, creates more fear and distrust of healthcare providers. We witness the stripping away of patients' rights and safety. The alarming power of the Mental Health Act becomes difficult to comprehend. Nothing in our family life has prepared us for what is unfolding.

I can feel my fingers losing their grasp, and everyone in the family tumbles into their own corner of denial. Each of us copes in our own way. British Columbia is about to declare a provincial public health emergency. We have a front-row seat to the deadly toxic drugs that are beginning to ravage a generation.

We feel completely alone.

Letters
September 3, 2016
Limon, Costa Rica

I am parked in the truck on a country road writing this on a scrap of paper, and my pen is running out of ink. There is sunshine, crickets, and the smell of dry, late-summer grass. I am thinking only of you.

I want to say so much to you, but words, as always, seem so futile. My heart is full of "everything you." I am watching sisters demonstrate unconditional love. I see a brother write a beautiful letter to his little sister. I see your father cry. Like a quilt with a few stitches out of place, it is still a quilt that is strong and warm. The worn patches are reminders of the rub of life. It might tear in places, but that does not mean that the quilt has lost its purpose or cannot be mended. It is a healing shroud of love we long to put over your shoulders.

You have had, without a doubt, a hard journey so far. I have been only able to observe. I want you to know that I often go out and scream at the ocean. About how unfair and cruel life has been. But then I think about all the tremendous courage you have shown me, especially this past year. Despite your pain, you pushed forward, and like a prize fighter, you tried to study, you found a few places to live, and you have relationships. You have always continued to be kind to all.

You are Pura Vida—a pure life.

There are many ways to ease pain and many ways that can heal your heart. Your beautiful heart. You are not the sum of terrible experiences. You are everything pura vida—our child, our daughter, our friend, our artist, our scholar, our beauty. An exceptional and resilient human being. I hope beautiful Costa Rica will provide a starting point to put your pain at peace. It is all part of your journey. And you are part of our journey. We can all do this together as people who share love in all its different forms—we just happen to be family. May you find the peace you need to complete yourself.

Love Mom

Waves of grief affect my husband and I differently. The strength of our marriage is duly tested. We must make more significant emotional and financial decisions based on limited information as we love our daughter from the sideline. I begin to write. From my kitchen table, I start a series of truthful letters based on reflection and encouragement. I find other ways to bring myself some measure of peace: prayer and meditation, saving hundreds of meaningful text messages and conversations between us, archiving email exchanges, filling up journals, researching addiction, attending alternative seminars, learning about harm reduction. I start sharing my heavy heart with strangers at support groups. I cannot breathe without safe places for my private feelings and the experiences of my family. One of the first letters I write is to our daughters travelling together across Costa Rica for an indefinite time of rest following a traumatic involuntary hospitalization spent in solitary confinement. We say heart-wrenching good-byes not knowing if she will return alive.

Eulogy
During the many sleepless nights, I find myself composing my daughter's eulogy. I want the world to know her as I do. To understand her struggle, her fight, her resilience, and her desire for a peaceful day and a creative life. No parent should ever have to pen their child's obituary. The possibility of losing her is a daily racing thought. The eulogy is our human way to make sense out of the senseless, a measure of preparedness. The feelings are bottomless. Nothing in my mind blames her for the pain we are enduring. Her hell is heartbreaking to us. We watch all our adult children struggle with their emotional lives. The sense of perpetual crisis, with the continuing rise of lethal drug poisonings being reported in the media, adds to our fear. I begin to recognize that we are grieving for ourselves, our children, and for the thousands of families and friends in mourning. Every night, I pray—I beg for her safety.

> *The garden dirt under my nails momentarily pushed away my sense of the world collapsing. It gave a flicker of hope that colour, bees, and sunshine would return to this landscape. One must be patient with all seasons to discover their purpose. My dirty fingers scroll the phone looking for a crumb of any news that she is alright and safe amongst the roaming wolves. I am on the highest alert, watching for danger at every turn of my head and every flick of a text posting. A mother bird looking into the forest should never be found writing her child's eulogy in the back of her heart.*
>
> *January 2017 – Anne's journal*

Let It Be
November 26, 2017
Victoria, British Columbia

Last week, when you texted me from the waterfront to say you had relapsed, I'll admit my heart sank. But when you said you were reading the letters from my kitchen table, it gave me hope. Right away, I started thinking that this setback would have a lot of lessons—hard lessons—and necessary lessons. It did not dash my hope. Your hope. Our hope.

I need to know you are safe and stable. I must take my father to Edmonton today and get him settled before we move. This is a huge event for him at this late stage of life. I don't think you are ready to leave treatment just yet. You are always in our hearts and minds. We have seen you journey a treacherous path.

Love Mom

Recovery in the addiction world has unique definitions of success. Relapse is part of healing and recovery. It has a personal way of sorting through the trauma, secrets, and expectations. It's a definition that changes as it becomes layered with pieces of hope and time. Healing is a slow process. I never expected to be on a journey of my own recovery and healing. I will strongly resist the notion that I will need to enter recovery myself to grow as a human being. All my deeply held expectations around abstinence will have to be released. Accepting measures of harm reduction will be the hardest change to make. Recovery will give me the opportunity to look at life and death, to rebuild trust, and to let go of grief while still holding hands with my daughter. Holding hands, not holding a hand. Caregiver, not caretaker. Daughter, not addict. Words matter. Hope matters.

Recovery is not a linear one-time experience.

It is my beloved elderly father who passes away a year after the wedding. In the spring of 2018, I am obliged to provide his health directive not to resuscitate. Dad, as his eulogy attested, was an intelligent and humorous source of wisdom for our family and much loved by all. As his caregiver in the final years of his life with us, I am grateful for so many engaging conversations and celebrations. When he learned about the struggles of his adult grandchildren, he was open about his battle with alcoholism as a young adult in his twenties, spending ten years drinking heavily until alcohol poisoning caused a near-fatal coma. He abstained from alcohol for the remainder of his life. He admitted that if he were a young person today, he would have tried everything. I grew up in a home of abstinence and conservative values. These lasting impressions carried into my generation of parenting. Dad was always surprisingly supportive. He offered non-judgmental guidance. His death was a poignant loss for our family, creating a significant turning point for me—perhaps for all of us—underscoring the fragility and preciousness of life.

We each have one life to live.

Slowly, in small ways, I start to find comfort by intentionally looking for beauty. I focus on gratitude. Whether I am planting a garden, journaling to declutter my mind, taking a photograph of my daughter's inked arm with the words **LET IT BE**, paddling the ocean in a kayak, making new memories of camping in a rain forest, or returning to my faith—it's all part of reclaiming things that bring life and joy. Self-awareness invites loosening that tight control of who we think we must be. It means acceptance of ourselves and our circumstances along the journey of healing. The outcome of my daughter's life is not in my hands.

Let it be.

> *Being in a garden feels more like God's presence than kneeling on my sore knees begging good things from God.*
>
> *May 2023 - Anne's journal*

Our family is learning that addiction will be part of our lifelong experience. We have different ways of coping with our own individual mental health issues. We agree that our youngest daughter's story of resilience and determination in recovery is exceptional. It takes courage to be honest and hopeful. We have learned, through the intersection of our lives, to accept harm reduction as the path forward for all of us. Through love and hope, healing has started to come into our lives. As my therapist and I work through my guilt around enabling, I gradually learn to let go of co-dependent patterns in my attempt to control outcomes. I wrestle with discerning what is helping or hindering my daughter. And myself.

As my sage counsellor says, "Ultimately, some situations require compassion."

Pandora
Acceptance has become the catalyst for change. Dr. Gabor Maté is a well-known Vancouver physician and author specializing in addiction and mental health with insights that are a balm in difficult times. He helps families explore their emotional lives and unhealthy patterns of communication. He imparts courage not to allow stigma to keep us from seeking treatment, counsel, and different expressions of recovery. Having an addiction is a medical diagnosis, not a moral or personal failing.

"The attempt to escape from pain, is what creates more pain." —Gabor Maté

Acceptance doesn't mean everything is okay. Accepting relapse, disability status, social assistance, food bank services, safe supply, and harm reduction; these require a deeper understanding and acceptance of the realities of addiction and mental illness. The drugs and supply are changing so rapidly that today's laws, policies, and health care services cannot keep up. Families often carry the burden of being primary caregivers in this ongoing public health emergency. Families are both frontline workers and advocates. And overdose responders. And the writers. Some things are NOT acceptable. Trying to stay normal when nothing is normal is unsustainable. Unregulated drug toxicity is now the leading cause of all deaths in British Columbia, as this unrelenting public health crisis grows and enters its sixth year.

Advocacy begins and ends with compassion. Becoming informed on the issues means learning about addiction and mental health. It's about the decision to be trained on how to administer the life-saving opioid overdose-reversing naloxone. These "free to the public" carry-kits are in my house and car. Naloxone has saved my daughter's life many times. Every time. She has, in turn, saved dozens of friends' and strangers' lives using naloxone. Advocacy includes grieving with my daughter when she receives tragic news again and again about another young friend who has died unnecessarily from fentanyl poisoning or suicide. The aftermath of the COVID pandemic has created more isolation, fear, anxiety, and vulnerable homeless people. Hardships have exasperated limited health and social services. Moms Stop the Harm, the prominent national advocacy group, offers compassionate support and lobbying efforts for families and loved ones facing this public health emergency. Sadly, the loss of thousands of loved ones has generated this strong, unstoppable voice. During stable periods of recovery, our daughter is a strong advocate and has worked tirelessly for Edmonton's Hope Mission shelter, AIDS Vancouver Island's harm reduction services, and for Our Place Society on Victoria's notorious Pandora Avenue, providing services to the most vulnerable. She bravely uses her voice to speak for the voiceless.

She knows both sides of the street.

Pandora, the first woman according to Greek mythology, opened the box containing all the misery of humanity, spilling out sickness, death, violence, and evil into the world. What most do not know is that only **Hope** is left inside Pandora's box, symbolizing resilience and optimism in the face of adversity. Homeless, broke, and existing out of her old car, our daughter's last overdose was on the formidable sidewalk of Pandora Avenue. We carried our daughter home because of the disgraceful lack of available medically supervised recovery beds and watched her painfully withdraw and detox from all the illegal and prescribed psychiatric drugs raking through her exhausted body.

> *Behind your quivering eyelids and sweat on your brow, there are nightmares and fears that I cannot enter nor dare to shake you awake. I imagine you are seeing yourself flying above this earth, then collapsing to the ground as that poison grabs your breath and squeezes until nothingness. When it is done with you, it spits you out.*

August 2023 – Anne's journal

Wildflower

Everyone arrives for the reunion. It is the first time in six years since the wedding that we are all in the same city. On their anniversary, our son and his wife fly in from France; our eldest daughter and her partner have returned to the family fold, and our youngest daughter, in a period of recovery, arrives with her dear friend. Grandfather is with us in spirit. This family reunion is long overdue. Relationships have suffered fractures, so we all agree it would be best to visit each other separately this time. To a mother and father, it's evidence that healing has started to mend the family. It is enough.

I am so proud of the kindness, forgiveness, and compassion that I see in our circle. Compassion literally means "to suffer together" and feel motivated enough to relieve that suffering.

A wildflower is resilient, beautiful, and can survive difficult conditions. My daughter's story is different from my story. But it is, after all, our story. Perhaps we are both wildflowers. My hope is that scattered in those many love letters, years of archived text messages, numerous notes, stacks of anxious journals, and photographs capturing rare moments of peace and joy—she knows she is loved. I have beautiful photographs of her floating on a green, sun-dappled salmon river, kayaking along a calm ocean shoreline, she and her beloved black dog smiling for my camera, and mom and daughter watching a Tofino sunset together. She is amazingly alive. And so am I. Hope does appear when we least expect it.

Hope is what we hold onto most during the worst and best days of addiction.

We are indebted to life-saving front-line workers, strangers, and brave friends who provide the gifts of harm reduction that save the lives of our loved ones. The growing support network of Holding Hope Canada gives families, like ours, a safe space to share our stories without stigma or shaming as we build resilience and resources in our communities. A new treatment option with buprenorphine is now offered through our local addictions clinic. It is a medically covered treatment and support for those with moderate to severe opioid addiction. By blocking opioid receptors in the brain, buprenorphine eliminates the overwhelming cravings and significantly reduces the chance of relapse. These prescribed monthly abdominal injections slowly release buprenorphine, which allows our daughter to **choose recovery** every 30 days. By replacing the agonizing decision of choosing recovery every single moment, the clinical team can carefully monitor and encourage our daughter towards a sustainable, stable, and continuous choice of health and life. Buprenorphine is still a relatively new, but promising treatment option. Our daughter is a brave and willing pioneer. Despite it all, she is living, working, and thriving. This kind of safe treatment provides dignity and a chosen "soberish life" on the harm reduction spectrum of her needs, as she calls it. Our family bears witness to the transformation of our precious daughter and sister, whom we so fondly call our wildflower.

Moment by moment, we move together with the hope of **our unfinished love story.**

> *Watching you sleep, there you are, finally back under my wing, curled up in your father's bed. I watch your face and tired body as you dream hard and fast. I hope for forests, swaying wildflowers, and floating in shimmering water. Wrapping you up in my arms, I cover you with your favourite quilt and watch you sleep into another day with us.*

August 2023 - Anne's journal

Everything Is (Not) Normal

by Heather Alexander

The pit of my little belly feels fluttery. It's almost my turn to take the stage. I get to be a police officer today and act like a boy! I've practiced my boy voice, and I know all my lines. Here I go; it's my turn... I can hear everyone laughing hysterically, and they are clapping, clapping for me.

There are so many people in this room; it's going to be hard to find my mom, but I will. So many smiling faces, so many hugs. Mine will come soon. Mom will be so proud... Where is she? There's no way she's not here. Dad was going to be home in time so she could come watch my school play. Someone had to watch my younger brother and sisters.

I'll find her.

"Sorry, dear, your mom asked me to take you home. She couldn't make it."

That voice inside to the rescue... *don't you dare cry! Don't you do it! Be strong! Do not show your disappointment; do not show your shame.* I shut it all off.

Dropped off at home, it's the same old, same old. Mom is mad, and Dad is drunk. I go directly to my bedroom. "You better go talk to your daughter."

I hear him coming to my room and then, through drunken slurs, "Look, dear, I'm sorry, I fucked up, I'm a terrible dad, I'm sorry."

I hate it. He's crying. I tell him, "It's okay; you're not a terrible dad." Head down; he stumbles out of my room. The door closes. I'm alone. It's safe. I cry.

Confused
I'm upstairs, and I hear a commotion. I'm supposed to be in bed, but I sneak out. Mom has answered the door. It's my dad, except he's not; he can barely talk, and there are two men holding him up. Their eyes are looking down, avoiding Mom's glare. Their faces hold pity and shame. I feel scared. Is my dad okay? Mom doesn't seem worried; her face is a mask of disgust and anger—again.

Self-Appointed Peacekeeper
Around seventh grade, unsolicited, I took on the responsibility to convince Dad to come home before Mom got off her afternoon shift. I dialed the local drinking hole and asked for him. They yelled out loud, "Is Dave here?" I could hear him brushing them off. The gruff voice came back on the line and bold-face lied to me.

I hang up. I give it time, I get creative, and I call back using the deepest version of my "man" voice I can find and ask again, curtly and deeply, "Is Dave there?" This time, he comes to the phone. "Come home," I beg, "Mom will be home soon."

"I'm coming home, dear," he promises. Sometimes he made it, other times he didn't. Same old, same old.

"Heather, the principal wants to see you."

My mind races: although I was mischievous and could be a handful, I was a rule-follower. The school counsellor is in the office. Their friendly faces are calm, but I'm confused.

"Hello Heather, we need to discuss your exam grades. Is everything okay at home?"

"Yes, everything is good. I studied but don't understand my grades."

"Are you sure there isn't anything at home that may be distracting you, maybe getting in the way of your studies?"

I pause and think about their question. *What do they mean by distraction?* Maybe they mean when I wait up trying to get Dad home before Mom gets off work. I share my story; no biggie to me. I'm quite certain it's normal for many kids, who are the oldest, to keep the peace. Right? I feel my answer is what they were looking for. They tell me about a youth group for kids whose parents drink. They give me pamphlets to take home and share with my parents. I like the idea—a chance to be social and hang out with other kids. Excited, I brought the brochures home. "Look. I've been invited!" Their faces told the story right away. My dad hung his head, and my mom, well, her frustration was as clear as day.

The idea died and the pamphlets disappeared. No ALATEEN for me. While visiting a friend's house, I mentioned to my friend that her dad was drunk— just a matter-of-fact statement.

"No, he's not!" she blurted out.

But later that evening, while playing hide-and-seek, I saw him pull a mickey out of the basement rafters and take a swig straight out of the bottle. I never said a word.

Mouthy Teen
I finally understood why Dad driving himself home was dangerous. I became self-righteous and what my parents referred to as "mouthy." The idea of my dad driving while impaired and killing someone terrified me. I just wanted him to stop. "I hope he kills himself before he kills someone I know." I didn't want him to die, but I was almost more afraid I'd be going to school with an orphan because of my dad.

Smitten Tomboy
At 14, I notice a boy, like really notice him. When we make eye contact, it feels like an unbearable lightness taking away all the normal dread. Was this love? I was learning to drink beer in boxcars, skip school, and roll a joint. Not with my friends, just his. In my community and school, I was the youngest to hold a position as a provincial executive for a group called Allied Youth, or AY for short. We'd have fun together developing leadership and interpersonal skills, self-awareness, and community involvement. It was for "good" kids. I played high school basketball and field hockey.

Despite being social, no one knew about my "boyfriend." I wasn't one of the girls that boys noticed in my community. Chances are, I'd already told a few off and popped a couple in the nose. I was not considered girlfriend-material.

***Adulting* Even More**
At 15 years old, I found myself pregnant. I was devastated. However, as I came to terms with what this truly meant—that I was growing a tiny body—I wanted so badly to keep this baby, but how? My inside voice spoke, *You're 15 stupid; it's not your decision to make. How are you going to feed, clothe, and pay for a baby? This isn't up to you; you don't get to decide.*

Please God, help me find a way.

My mom figures it out. I just had a knock-down, drag-out yelling match, butting heads with my dad, and crying. I don't cry.

She sternly asks, "What's the matter with you?"

"It's bad, Mom."

"How many months?"

"Three," I sobbed.

We aren't sure how to tell Dad, but when the benefit concert night arrives, it's clear it's time.

I had been the main organizer to raise funds for a local charity. I felt like I was juggling a hundred tasks at once. My heart pounded, not just with excitement but with the secret I carried—a secret only my mother and boyfriend knew.

The evening ended as a huge success. As I moved backstage, I felt a gentle nudge from within. I rested a hand on my belly, hidden beneath my loose blouse. My mother stood nearby. Her presence was a silent support, reminding me I wasn't alone.

Just as I turned to say goodbye to one of the performers, my foot caught on a stray cable. Time seemed to slow as I stumbled, reaching out for something to grab onto but finding nothing. I fell down the stairs, my body hitting each step with a sickening thud. Pain shot through me, and I gasped, clutching my stomach protectively.

The bustling backstage area went silent. Faces blurred as people rushed to help me. My mother's face appeared, her eyes wide with fear, but her voice steady. "Heather, are you alright?" I was physically fine; however, my feelings were bruised with embarrassment. As the saying goes, I went "ass over teakettle" down the flight of stairs.

Later, once at home, Mom took a deep breath, her eyes serious. "Heather, we need to tell your father. He deserves to know. If anything had happened to you or the baby, he would be devastated. We can't keep this secret any longer."

I nodded. Relief and fear waged a battle inside me. The secret would be out, and so would the consequences. It was time to face whatever came next.

"I will tell your father tonight."

Relieved
I dodged my dad for the next few days until he finally found me alone. "I know what's going on. What are you going to do?"

He's asking me? I was the kid.

"Dr. Ash says I should give the baby up."

"No way! That baby is as big a part of me as it is of you. That baby is staying right here in this home. You're not the first. You sure as hell won't be the last. I don't give a fuck what anybody thinks."

The words were exactly what I prayed for.

The plan was that once the baby was born, we were all moving, including my boyfriend.

I gave birth on June 11th to a beautiful six-pound, one-and-a-half-ounce baby boy. I named him David Scott. He had the darkest, most beautiful eyes I'd ever seen.

I was adamant that I would be *the* mom. I woke up at 3 a.m. for him. I wanted to do all the feedings, the diaper changes, the baths—everything. As soon as school ended, we moved from PEI all the way to Edmonton, in central Alberta.

My mom and three younger siblings were incredible, eager to help at every turn. They hovered, always ready to swoop in and take over a feeding, a diaper change, or simply hold him while I caught a few minutes of sleep. I would be the one he knew was always there, even in the dead of night. September loomed. Already mid-July, and in just a couple of months, I'd have to return to school. The thought of leaving him, only three months old, even for a few hours, made my heart ache.

Yet, I knew school was the only route to providing a better life for us. What if he rejected me and chose my mom as his whole world? What if I couldn't wake up for school after his nightly feeding?

My boyfriend, Scott, a teen dad, was also struggling. He'd grown up in a small community, and bustling, noisy Edmonton felt like a cage. His frustration was palpable. "We need to go back," his voice tinged with desperation. "This place isn't for us."

But it wasn't just about us—it was about our son, too. I made calls, my heart pounding. "Can I legally leave home at 16 and take my son out of the province?" I'd ask, bracing myself for the answer. Finally, when I confirmed that I could, a sense of relief washed over me.

We started to plan, whispering while the house slept. We mapped out our route, saved what little money we had, and prepared for the journey. The hardest part was telling my parents.

That evening we broke the news, my mom's face went pale, and my dad's jaw clenched. I braced myself for the storm.

"You're only sixteen," my dad said, his gruff voice a mix of anger and worry. "You can't be serious."

I squared my shoulders, keeping my voice steady. "We've made up our minds. We hate it here. We need to go back."

As certain as a bullheaded teenager can be, I couldn't understand why they were angry, afraid, disappointed, and resistant. Now, looking back, I see their concern as their deep love and a desire to protect us. But I was determined, blinded by my need to take control of our lives and do what I thought was best.

As we finished packing, I felt a mixture of excitement and trepidation. But I was ready to face the uncertain road ahead. I believed in our plan and was confident we could make it work.

Reality hit me like a cold wave as I woke up with my son in our tiny apartment back on PEI. The early light filtered through the cracked blinds, casting long shadows across the room. My son gurgled softly from his crib, and I forced myself out of bed, the weight of my exhaustion settling heavily. As I held my son close, feeling his warmth and listening to his soft breaths, I tried to summon the strength to face another day.

I warmed a bottle, my mind already racing. Juggling homework, diapers, and feedings, I often slept on the pull-out couch while Scott and his friends partied in the kitchen.

Last night, I heard Scott return around 2 a.m., the door creaking softly, followed by hushed voices and footsteps. My heart sank. I knew. The money he brought home, the whispers, the strangers coming and going—all pointed to one thing. He was dealing.

Fear gnawed at me constantly. What if the authorities found out? What if they discovered my baby in an environment like this?

The final straw came when my son was hospitalized for a flu bug. I was spending all my time at the hospital, until one night I had a friend spell me off. Arriving home, a group of strange faces stared back through a haze of smoke, laughing and shouting. Scott stood cramped in the corner, his eyes vacant.

That night, I lay awake, my mind spinning. I couldn't risk my son's safety. The realization was like a punch to the gut. Deciding to leave tore at my heart. Despite everything, I still loved Scott. But my love for my son trumped all else.

When Scott came to the hospital, I told him I couldn't let our son be exposed to the dangers that came with his lifestyle. I wished things could be different and that he could see the harm he was causing.

As he stood, waiting for the elevator, he pleaded, "Please don't do this to us."

It crushed me, but my childhood skill at stoppering up the dam of emotions reigned again. I waited for the elevator doors to close and once he was gone, the tears came in a hot, unstoppable torrent. Each sob tore through me, gut-wrenching and raw, as if my soul was a razor of pain slicing me inside. This time, I could no longer contain the grief in a neat package behind closed doors.

Back with my son in my arms, I took a deep breath. But as I looked down at his tiny fingers wrapped around mine, I knew parenting alone was my path. That didn't make it any easier. Dropping my son off at daycare and picking him up, I stretched a $593 monthly social assistance cheque. Right off the top, $350 paid the rent. That left me with a meagre $243 for utilities, groceries, clothing, diapers, and laundry. Forget entertainment and TV dinners. Bottle-collecting with a sleigh or stroller provided funds for small extras. Studying had to fit in while rocking my son, or while he was sleeping. I did what it took and earned my Grade 12 diploma at 18.

Post-secondary was a wake-up call. Feeling defeated, I called my dad, "I surrender."

"I'm buying you a plane ticket. Come home."

Instead of feeling shame, I felt taken care of. Once again, my parents stepped up. With family support, I worked and pursued my post-secondary education. I met my husband, Hugh, while working with incarcerated youth. We married the same year Scott lost his life to addictions. He was 26.

Hugh legally adopted David, and for the next fourteen years, my little family enjoyed stability—jobs, vacations, weekends in the rink, or on the ball diamond watching David. Hugh also played hockey, so our social life fell into a routine of parties and lots of booze!

It was fun until it wasn't! As the years passed, resentment grew like a tumour. I truly believed that this is just what boys do: they work hard, and they play hard. Late night drinking, not coming home when they say they will, and worrying about them driving impaired. The swing from anger to worry. Wondering at 3 a.m., will he make it home alive.

For years, I truly believed I was the abnormal one; I'm the problem because I'm not cut out to be *the good wife*, keep the peace, and be tolerant. It wasn't up to me to try to make things different. Who was I to rob him of his "happy?" Clearly, life was working for him. It was time to make another tough decision. This time, I chose me.

My fear of starting over diminished as the pain of my reality ballooned like a mushroom cloud.

After countless discussions, okay, mostly arguments about his drinking, I hit a wall. *I realized it's not my place to interfere with what brings him joy. It's not my responsibility. I will be responsible for me.* I was done being angry with the booze, the circumstances, and the fear of him driving impaired. Anger served only as a weak façade for helplessness. I can't change anyone. I could barely stand myself in my own skin. I was done with our cyclical fighting, make-up, same old, same old...

Though we didn't separate; we healed through coaching. Both of us committed to NOT consuming alcohol. Yes, both of us. Although I never had a dependency on it, it had brought me tremendous pain. A coach suggested, "If you're sick and tired of the alcohol in your life, perhaps you need to be the first to remove it."

It was the wisest support I've ever received. It starts with you. "The good news is, 'this is all about you,' and the bad news is, 'this is all about you.'"

I've spent a lifetime normalizing addictions. I gave myself the gift of therapy. Shocked, the therapist referred to my experiences as trauma. "Oh gosh, NO, you misunderstand. Do you really think that just because I grew up around addiction, it fits the definition of true trauma? That feels excessive."

She loaned me a book... who knew there was an entire book describing my feelings, beliefs, and experiences.

Does the word trauma feel too much for you? Trauma was later explained to me as when we experience stressful, frightening, or distressing events that are difficult to cope with or are beyond our control. By that definition, although still somewhat uncomfortable, I am learning to accept this as truth.

I am not now, nor have I ever felt like a victim. However, here's the problem with my thinking: Not wanting to be perceived as a victim has negatively impacted my ability to heal. Minimizing my experiences meant I wasn't fully acknowledging the impact on my mental and emotional well-being. I dug in hard, and by refusing to recognize myself as a victim, internally, I held shame and self-loathing.

I realized avoiding the label of "victim" had me suppressing emotions and prevented me from processing trauma. If I stayed in this belief system, it was the equivalent of signing up for a crash course in "Mental Instability 101" with full instructions on "how to stick your head further up your ass." By mastering the art of being around substance abuse, perfecting the art of avoidance, and becoming so emotionally detached, I could have given an AI robot a run for its money.

Seeking help required me to acknowledge my own vulnerability and accept assistance from others, which dumped an iron knot in my stomach.

By acknowledging my experiences and seeking appropriate support, I was able to undo the knot and support others to do the same unravelling in their lives. It's about claiming our resilience and getting the heck out of our own way so we may create the life of our dreams.

Life is constant growth; I don't know what I don't know. From a smoke-filled life of poverty in a tiny apartment, I now encounter moments where awe at my life strikes like lightning with gratitude. Bravely stepping into places outside of my norm, one hundred percent, is what contributed to my healing. Gratitude is my touchstone for each moment. It can be yours too.

My story speaks to those who believe they haven't been touched by addiction, thinking this book is for others—those directly battling addiction or living in its shadow. I once thought the same. During a phone call, when I was invited to participate in this book, I hesitated. I even said out loud, "I don't know if I'm a fit." My friend paused, and the silence on the line spoke volumes.

"But I'm okay," I thought. "I'm not an addict. Others have it worse. I have a great life. But, but, but..." I had dismissed and normalized my experiences, replaying them until they felt ordinary, all I had ever known.

Her pause revealed the many ways addiction had threaded throughout my life as I took a quick inventory of my life. Addiction had been present since birth. My father, a hard-working man, the life of every party with his colourful tales, and our fierce protector, was a functional alcoholic.

My first boyfriend, my first love, forced to take on responsibility way beyond his young years, was addicted to drugs, and died of an overdose at 26.

Believing I knew better, I swore I would never end up in a relationship with someone struggling with alcohol or drugs. Yet, after 16 years of marriage, I had to confront the truth: I had married my father. Not literally, but a man who drank too much, and it was taking its toll on my life.

My story is for those where addiction has lurked on the edges, seeping into the cracks, fraying the fabric of our peace, and how to reclaim our birthright to joy.

www.gratocoaching.com

It Ain't No Movie

by Callum Roth

From my early teenage years in the late '90s, I was obsessed with the drug culture. I was fascinated by it. The rich and famous were indulging in it, adding to the glorification. Gangster and prison movies were dominating the film industry... I wanted to live it.

You could say it all began when I was 17 and I took my rebellious phase to the extreme. I was in my third year at a private Christian school, on the verge of graduating, and dating the principal's daughter. One night, while stoned and tubing down the river just meters from her house, I dropped in on her. When she confronted me and said, "I don't want to date a guy who's smoking pot," I broke up with her on the spot. This was my first breakup, and it was one that my addiction chose for me. From that point on, my addiction drove everything away.

Within forty-eight hours, I was expelled from school. My parents, fed up with my weed-smoking, gave me an ultimatum: quit or move out. I chose to move out. I was determined to prove myself as an adult. When I discovered that underage kids couldn't apply for or receive welfare, I convinced myself I didn't need anyone's help. I would make a go of it on my own. I was a man! My older brother, who was working in Vancouver, helped me land a job renovating mansions. Another friend hooked me up with an apartment.

Everything went smoothly for about two months—until I started drinking every day after work and met some new people. I also began exploring other job opportunities.

One day, a production manager offered me a job doing security at the raves he organized. During a break at one of these events, I sat in my car with other staff members as they passed around a pipe. They called it *jib*.

"What's that?" I asked.

"It's like a cup of coffee," one of them replied with a laugh. I would later learn that *jib* was street slang for methamphetamine.

My first thought after hitting the pipe was just, "Wow." I was so stoned, yet wide awake. Over the next four months, I lost about 100 pounds, which made me feel amazing. Being overweight had always made me self-conscious. Almost instantly, I started selling the drug, making more money than I ever thought possible. Girls started hanging out with me, and suddenly, I had this incredible sex life.

It felt like I was the main character in a movie that glorified the drug culture—sex, drugs, selling drugs, stealing drugs, doing armed robberies for drugs, robbing other drug dealers, and having other drug dealers rob me. Life was insane, yet I kept telling myself, "I love this life."

Go, Stop, Relapse
There was no stopping me. By the time I hit my late twenties, I was into opiates, and by 30, I was a full-blown intravenous drug addict. That action-packed movie I was the star of was about to become a sorrowful tragedy.

It was then that I realized I had a serious problem. I started to seek answers and educate myself on addiction, and I learned it was a disease. I went to Baldy Hughes Therapeutic Community and Farm, a private addiction treatment centre located in Prince George, British Columbia. This was the first time someone actually broke it down for me and explained the disease of alcoholism and drug addiction.

Unfortunately, I used what I learned the wrong way. Is there a wrong way? Everyone is different. Maybe you cannot learn anything the wrong way; you can only really learn it the way YOU learn it. I learned it the hard way. I believed I could control my drug use. I figured if I understood my enemy, if my enemy was addiction, and if I learned everything about it, then I could control it.

But that was a lie.

Between the ages of 30 and 36, I would attend 18 different rehabs. I was in and out of treatment centres and facilities, hospitals, and prisons, blind to the symptoms of this disease. I sought out different methods of communicating and talking about it, looking for trauma therapy. I dabbled in the 12 steps of Alcoholics Anonymous, Narcotics Anonymous, and Cocaine Anonymous, doing bits and pieces of all these programs, but never actually working them. I just went through the motions, taking the tools that suited my ongoing obsession, but that didn't work out for me.

It was a constant go, stop, relapse. Go. Stop. Relapse. Go. Stop. Relapse. Get clean. Go for two days. Get clean. Go. Stop. Relapse. For a week. Get clean. Relapse. Go for two or three months. Relapse.

The High Toll
My life was dictated by the selfish ways of the disease: manipulation, lies, crimes I committed, and high tolls of street violence. Despite the physical exhaustion, I kept telling myself, *This is the life I want. This is what it's all about, like in the movies. Chicks dig scars. Don't worry about getting your face all fucked up. They'll be into it. Don't worry if someone smashes your teeth out; buy new ones.*

This was my delusion.

Living in Calgary, when I was 30, I rented a full three-bedroom house with a two-bedroom basement suite on the northeast side of the city. I hadn't paid rent for four months. I called my parents and said, "I am an intravenous heroin user and desperately need your help." I wanted to head west.

To fund my escape, I sold off possessions and stolen merchandise and collected as much money as possible. My plan was to buy a truck and trailer, pack up my girlfriend, dogs, and everything I owned, and then head out to the West Coast to fight for my life for the first time. This plan set off a wild 42-day spree to make as much money as I could, culminating in regrettable actions.

Right before leaving, I rented out the entire house, both the upstairs and the basement suite, collecting the first and last month's rent for both units, totalling around $10,000. In the basement suite, a young mother with a newborn baby, supported by her father, moved in. Meanwhile, a family with two teenage boys took the upstairs. I knew I didn't own the house and was merely using the money to fund my escape, leaving behind a mess for others to clean up. Despite the guilt, I cashed their checks, sold every last saleable item, loaded my truck and trailer, and fled from the chaos that had become my life.

These events were precipitated by the murder of the drug dealer I had been working for, intensifying the fear and instability I felt. I had a $1500/day drug habit and was involved in cooking crystal meth for an organization, making $30,000 a week. However, with the death of that dealer, the easy money disappeared, and I couldn't afford my addiction. I fled toward the West Coast, embarking on a new, uncertain adventure.

Kidnapped, Beaten, Tortured
I was 33 years old, living in Comox Valley, and successfully running a drug shack. Financially, I was doing okay, managing to provide for my habit while living a squalid life. I was barely sober. Another person in the drug culture had their house broken into, and a couple of their guns were stolen. The victim, suspecting me, believed I had either bought or stolen these guns.

We met in a public place early on a Friday morning. There were four of them, and I was alone. I told them I had no idea about the guns, which was the truth, and they let me walk away. Later, I received a phone call; they wanted to meet again to discuss the situation. Desiring to prove my innocence, I agreed. A friend of mine, who also ran a drug shack in Campbell River, drove me to an empty parking lot on Ham Road on Vancouver Island. He seemed scared, which should have been a warning.

As soon as we pulled into the lot, our car was surrounded by four guys. I was dragged out of the car and beaten. They also pulled someone else out of another vehicle's trunk, someone they believed I had hired to steal the guns. This person had sold me a legitimate shotgun unrelated to the stolen ones, but they assumed I was involved.

Both of us were beaten, then threatened with a chainsaw, demanding we reveal the location of the guns. Despite the fear, I insisted I had nothing to do with the theft. They took us along, shoving us into the back of a small car, heading for another drug house, seeking to recover the guns. My tailbone and ribs were aching from the beating.

They drove to the drug house, hoping the guns were there. My co-accused managed to escape when one of the captors needed to relieve himself. At 1 a.m., he flagged down the driver of a passing car, who called 911. Meanwhile, I was terrified and incapable of getting out of the car, going into a serious state of shock.

As we neared Courtney, seeing police and ambulances heading to the scene, my captors panicked. They met up on a dark road and decided it was best to release me. I exchanged phone numbers with them, assuring them I wouldn't talk to the cops.

I walked to my parents' home, which happened to be a few blocks away, grateful to be alive. My body was in shock from the injuries: four broken ribs, a dislocated shoulder, and a fractured tailbone. I didn't go to the hospital for seven days. The next day, the cops showed up. I told them repeatedly that I was home watching Netflix. My co-accused had already spoken to them, but I held fast to my lie, fearing for my life and my credibility in the drug culture.

My parents saw my injuries and helped me, but the cops kept pressing for information. Eventually, the co-accused overdosed and died, leaving no witness. The police wanted to charge the kingpin behind the kidnapping, but without my testimony, they couldn't proceed. This man still walks free today.

The police were relentless, harassing me every day. My addiction threw debris all over my family. My parents laid down some clear boundaries. It was not long after my harrowing experience of being kidnapped and tortured that I fled from Comox Valley. I tried to find refuge in Vancouver, hoping to get clean and spare my family, but also to hide from them. Unfortunately, I relapsed after leaving the treatment centre and ended up at the Grand Union dive right on Hastings. If those 130-year-old walls could talk, they would tell horrific stories. I hung out there until I was sent to prison.

Released from Prison
Convicted for selling fentanyl, I survived until my prison release in August 2020. After being locked up for 14 months, my family begged me to come

home. I had been sober for at least the last six months of my jail sentence, and my family wanted to see me. But with a completely straight mind, I told them I couldn't come home because that would put me too close to my brother. He was three months sober at that time and living with my parents. I said if I was anywhere near my brother, we'd end up high together, and it wouldn't be fair to him.

I made the hard decision to go straight from Wilkinson Road provincial jail in Victoria, BC, back to downtown Hastings in Vancouver... back into the *fire*. This is where the perfect storm started to brew. In a complete, sober state in jail, I believed I was destined to die a junkie death. It broke something inside me to tell my family that I couldn't come home. I was already jonesing for the drugs I'd hidden in the outfit that the prison stored for me for my release. Before my arrest, I had placed meth in the rolls of my full-length jeans, bought specially from a thrift store for this purpose. Of course, they checked my pockets when they took my clothes and gave me the prison gear, but they never touched the folds of the jeans that I'd made into shorts by rolling up the pant legs. Released, I got high within 35 feet of the exit before my mom even picked me up in the parking lot. That's the sad truth. I was itching so bad just to escape the devastating experience of being in prison for 14 months that I could not stop myself.

My mom took me out for lunch. It was nice to see her. To this day, I don't know if she knew I was high. Probably. Mothers normally do. She sent me on my way to Vancouver, and I continued using, descending into what I'd now call *my last tear*. I went at it hard and fast.

I had accumulated money while in prison, enough to go on a really decent run. Off I went, deep and hard, right around the same time that benzodiazepine was entering the street drug scene. I would have two, three, or four-day blackouts from it and wake up missing articles of clothing and covered in my own urine in foreign places, with cuts, bruises, and burns of unknown origins. Often, I didn't even remember my own name—that was terrifying. My ability to take care of myself was zero. To shower, brush my hair, and do the most basic things became monumental challenges that I failed to overcome.

I couldn't make it to doctor's appointments or go get methadone. There were times when the street drugs incapacitated me to the point where I couldn't even cross the street to the pharmacy to get the methadone to help me get through. My ability to function decreased when I couldn't get enough street drugs; I'd sink into failure to thrive. By the fall of 2020, I'd been doing drugs for so long that dipping in and out of a drug-induced psychosis was my normal state. The amount of methamphetamine I injected in my veins and inhaled through my lungs, on top of the fentanyl and benzodiazepines, all mixed together, has a street name: *tranq* dope. On top of the crack cocaine and any other mind-altering drugs I put in my system, I embarked on the fast path of impending self-destruction.

As I slipped deeper and deeper into this psychosis, my debts to former drug dealers haunted me. Every tinted window vehicle, everyone who looked at me—they were all coming for me—to grab me, bag my head, zip-tie me, drag me away, and I'd never see my family again. I'd seen it happen to other druggies. That fear took over, and logic disappeared.

Lonely, Terrifying Life
The loneliness I felt was overwhelming, compounded by the nostalgia of when I was at the top of my game. My life was a blur of money and drugs, but no amount of wealth could buy me happiness. No amount of thinking that I could control my addiction led to triumph.

As my addiction progressed, I found myself surrounded by other lost, beautiful souls. Living on Hastings was a terrifying ordeal. The dope was getting stronger, and the fear of owing money to dangerous people was ever present. Hastings was a place where survival was uncertain. The combination of meth and fentanyl, along with mental health issues, drug politics, and the violence of the streets, dumped me into deeper and deeper states of psychosis. I was hallucinating and hearing voices. I was certain I could hear guns being loaded and the click of a safety released. Every doorway was a potential threat, hiding people out to get me. This period of my life was marked by paranoia and fear. I barricaded myself in a dilapidated apartment at the Grand Union just off Hastings, overrun by cockroaches and rats, convinced I was being hunted.

The psychosis dominated every waking moment. I was convinced that people from my past were coming to settle old debts, and I lived in a perpetual state of terror. My hallucinations were so vivid that I could hear people loading guns and whispering about coming to get me. I was trapped in my mind, unable to distinguish reality from delusion.

No one was safe. I watched body after body after body be taken out of that building. I just figured I'd be one of them. Each time the psychosis took me hostage, it plunged me deeper, negating all reality. If I did manage periods of lucidity, the psychosis took over, stealing two or three weeks at a time, plummeting me into the abyss again and again.

I missed my brother. He was the only one who could break through the paranoia. The drug culture pulled him in, too. It was a terrifying time in my life, witnessing his twisted journey that, for a time, paralleled mine. Both of us haunted Hastings Street, which in turn haunted us via our obsession with the next high. Back then, he was the only one I could hear or trust when lost in psychosis, and, crucially, he was the one who convinced me I needed hospital care. Now, without him, survival teetered on the edge of eternal darkness. Before prison, he was my lifeline.

He became an intravenous drug user before me, which was frightening. Our paths continued to intertwine and diverge, but we were always connected. As I healed from my own struggles between the ages of 30 and 36, going through numerous treatment centres, he sought his path to recovery. Both of us were fighting for our lives and educating ourselves about the disease.

Our mother watched as her two sons cycled in and out of treatment, medical detox, hospitals, and even life support. The trauma mounted—broken backs, spinal injuries, surviving kidney failure. Our parents tried everything to support us, but eventually, we all realized that their efforts were enabling rather than helping. They continued to keep close tabs on us despite our chaotic lives on the street.

Fearing it might be my final Christmas, my family reached out. Even with their emotions sanded raw and despite their strict stance against drug use in their home, my parents invited me home, desperate to see me. Their fear was justified. Would I make it to 2021?

Christmas 2020
The drugs disrupted our family's tenuous tether but never broke the closeness we had for each other. My brother was at home and clean. I asked about their rule of not using drugs when they invited me to come home for Christmas.

"We just want you home for Christmas." My mother's voice broke. It must have been overwhelming for her to witness her sons flirting with death, unable to help us.

I went home. There wasn't enough dope in the world to help me through the holidays. I came with as much as I could. That Christmas, I was covered with open wounds and blow torch burns on my stomach from falling asleep with a lit torch between my legs. When family members dropped by or met me on video chat, they'd see the shape I was in: my mental health was zero. My physical health was gone. They'd start crying, and I would too. To me, it felt like my family members were saying goodbye.

I returned to downtown Vancouver the day after Boxing Day, and the next six weeks hurled me into even darker corners of my psyche. My psychosis took a deep dive overboard. I said goodbye to everyone, as I was losing my ability to care. I took new risks, like sharing needles.

I was racking up drug debts everywhere and failing at everything except being a suicidal weapon of mass consumption. Still, I couldn't escape my internal reality, finally admitting to myself: *I don't have a fentanyl problem, a crack cocaine problem, a methamphetamine problem, or an alcohol problem. I have a serious Callum problem.* I believed the only solution to my Callum problem was all those drugs. I used them all for their different ways of hiding from the *fire* that burned inside me.

Still, I didn't know any other way: I continued to treat my trauma, resorting over and over to my "drug" solution, getting sicker and sicker, mentally, physically, psychologically, and spiritually—totally morally depleted. I was hopeless...

On February 10, 2021, I barricaded myself in my bedroom, hallucinating, hearing guns clicking, and convinced that people outside my doorway were unfolding tarps and starting chainsaws. When I saw my oldest brother show up on social media at 6:30 in the morning, I asked him to call 911. He didn't know what to do or if what I was telling him was real or not real. I can't blame him based on my history. Hamish confirmed the chainsaws after talking with the apartment building manager. I was desperate to exit the room safely. The police arrived, asking if I wanted to make a police report or go to the hospital. I chose the hospital.

Standing by the cop car waiting for the ambulance was horrible. For 45 minutes, I faced public shaming. People pointed at me, yelling, "Snitch" because I had called the cops. By the time the ambulance arrived to take me to the hospital, I was in full-blown psychosis and twelve hours into withdrawal.

I went to the psych ward screaming that anyone giving me drugs was trying to kill me.

I was placed on a 72-hour floor, which was chaotic. Many people were coming and going. Drugs were prevalent. I didn't feel safe. Over and over, I told the doctors and nurses, "There are people trying to give me fentanyl. They are trying to kill me." On the third day, they finally moved me to a more secure floor with no drugs. I began to unwind. This time was different. This was the first time I chose not to take drugs. This was the first time I chose Callum.

Then, I was moved to the eighth floor, an even more secure wing. I was able to breathe, fully unbinding how tightly wound I'd been. For years, even though I was sober in prison, I was still enmeshed in the drug scene; I was always under pressure, always looking over my shoulder. Living as I had with a constant flow of drugs and no food or sleep, I was malnourished, and my brain was on hyperdrive. On the eighth floor, I put my hands up and began to surrender to all the damage I'd done.

Recovery
Coming off methamphetamine, fentanyl, and benzodiazepines was horrific. It took me almost twelve days to regain basic motor skills. I stayed in the hospital for over 34 days before they started pushing me out the door. I was on a waitlist for a treatment centre, but it wasn't ready for me, and the hospital insisted I leave. Desperate, I called my family, who helped me stay safe for a month while waiting for treatment. During this time, I got glasses and some identification and voluntarily stayed on lockdown.

Turning Point Vancouver was my 19th treatment center, having failed to complete 18 others in the six years prior. Despite my doubts, I was desperate and willing to try anything. Having another addict guide me through the 12 steps of Alcoholics Anonymous, one-on-one, brought me relief from my obsession with drugs for the first time. It was the first time I felt the *fire* go out and the first time I felt comfortable in my own skin.

Recovery was everyday work and required me to be vigilant and continue working the 12-step program. The obsession with drug use faded. I see a trauma counsellor for the sexual trauma I experienced from 7 until I was 9. I see an Opiate Agonist Therapy (OAT) doctor who is an addiction specialist and also helps with underlying mental health stuff. It takes a whole team working together to help me stay sober for a day at a time. It's a baffling disease. I'm so grateful. The whole process is much broader than me just not doing drugs.

Completing the six-month program was a huge accomplishment. I was now eight months sober, the longest ever. Returning home, I was still scared and didn't trust myself, so I stayed in my parents' basement for another five or six months. Gradually, I built confidence. At around 14 months sober, I got a job opportunity through an addictions clinic. Working two days a month, I began to regain stability in my recovery. Eventually, I started working full-time at the clinic, helping other addicts and alcoholics.

Today, I work at a pharmacy specializing in OAT therapy for vulnerable people. The 12 steps have given me freedom from my addiction. Each milestone I achieved, like getting my driver's license or a job, was accompanied by fear that I would mess it up. But now, after spending time helping others in my community, I know I will never again drink or do drugs. I am in remission. With the right daily practices, I can keep the obsession at bay. I feel free from the chains of addiction and hope my story can also help others find freedom. Today, I am recovered and recovering by staying active in working one-on-one with other men and journeying with them through the steps.

www.facebook.com/callum.roth

In the World of an Indian Woman

by Yiktsa7: Carol Thevarge

I find it difficult to explain
  Genocide
    Exploitation
      Oppression
without anger flooding and shedding the tears of my ancestors.

In the world of oppression, colonization imposed upon my people.
   The reign of terror still runs deep in my subconscious.
     In the subtlest ways... today, I re-enact my grandmother's past:

Her unspoken fear of men
  Her strength
    Her beauty that could not be expressed
      Her knowing that one day Indian Women would rise again.

She waits patiently
  I may not feel it
    I may not see it
      it is here within me every day.

Christianity tied our Indian men's hands behind their backs

> BEAT YOUR WOMEN!!!
>   HIT YOUR CHILDREN!!!

Our fathers
  hit,
    abused,
      controlled,
Families through rough dogmatic principles contradicting our forefathers' ways!!!

Christianity imposed and imposes many things upon my people.
  they have raped
    abused our children
      our minds
        our lands

They have taken our dignity and family values and turned us into their image!
  They have
    lied
      cheated
        stolen...
Is that an honourable way of life...?

Unfortunately, it has infected our way of life for many of our people today. In the shadow of the church, men and women are incarcerated for what residential schools forced into them.

Women are imprisoned for defending their children's lives
  Taking the lives of their men who have hurt them!
WHO WILL HEAR THEIR CRY!?!?

Our sacredness spit on.
  Our beauty painted with our own blood
    Our power shamed, demoralizing our very existence.
WHO WILL HEAR OUR CRY!?!?

My heart sings with sorrow for those who've travelled on to the spirit world
  those who found beauty in the earth
    peace in another dimension

Let's come together and walk this path of
  Love
    Light
      Freedom

Let's join hands and sing in harmony once again

Today, I call upon my Ancestors to help create new
  Thoughts
    Feelings
      Positivity

We will not allow
  Segregation
    Degradation
      Genocide...
  We will practice what we know works

LOVE...

All My Relations, Yiktsa7

In the World of an Indian Woman

I had no idea what the Creator had in store for me when I first sobered up. I had my first taste of alcohol when I was twelve years old after my mom and dad separated. My cousin and I were living with my late auntie across the lake in a little red house where the water froze all the time. It was winter when we filled an old mason jar with every kind of booze she had in her cabinet and took it to school with us to drink on a ski trip at Whistler's Little Rainbow Ski Hill. I remember not liking the feeling of alcohol in my system. I sat in the ski check-in building all day after one ski run. However, in my teen years, I sought out booze every chance I got, from stealing booze at weddings and adult gatherings to spending what little money I earned to buy tequila and a bag of lemons. On the reserve, it was normal to drink at such a young age. If you didn't, you were a goody-two-shoes. You were called chicken, and the others worried you'd tell on them. We watched our parents and followed their lead.

When I was 23, and my first child was two years old, I found myself stealing a car from guys I met at a rodeo dance. They promised to take me home after the dance, but they stopped at the riverside to help someone who had driven off the old dirt road right into the river. They left the car running, and I jumped into the front seat and peeled out of there. I drove about two kilometres before I flipped the car at the edge of a swamp. I crawled out of the wrecked car and walked back to a friend's house, all bloody and sore. She put me in a bath, washed my clothes, and then helped me sober up. It took about four days for the police to find me. The officer honked the horn out front of the house where I was living at the time, right after I smoked a joint—of course. He had me sit in the car with him while he reviewed what I had done. I did not deny it.

I had to go to Squamish to see the Crown Council by the end of the week. They were the first ones to tell me to get my shit together. I was damn lucky that the owner of the car chose not to press charges.

Crown Council questioned, "What are you going to do with the rest of your life?" That was the first time anyone had ever asked me what I wanted out of life. I went on to college in the fall. That is where I met the man who would become the father of my two sons. We drank together for six years. We would be drinking all weekend, passed out, or hung over on holidays. Some nights, we would have friends over to gamble and play poker. Everyone would bring their own booze. We would put the kids to bed, then gamble and drink in the dining room, our voices getting louder and louder. The last straw was when the two of us got in the car to make a beer run to town. It was Valentine's Day; we left the kids with my cousin. My partner, drunk, of course, ended up driving the car into a ditch after slipping on ice while cutting a corner too fast. Another accident, and this time, I woke up on a couch in a stranger's house with my shoes soaked and my feet freezing, feeling ashamed and guilty. I was on the Band Council, for Christ's sake! I couldn't hide my alcoholism anymore.

I went to Tsow-Tun Le Lum, "Helping House," an Aboriginal Drug and Alcohol Treatment Center in Nanaimo. Cultural and spiritual beliefs are integrated into a six-week program. I distinctly recall it being January, cold, and snowy. I had to ride across on a ferry, and surprised, I met my first cousin and her friends. They were going to the same treatment facility! *Oh, my gawd! I can't believe this… can I be vulnerable if I am in the same group as them?*

Wow! I was shocked again. My neighbour's partner was also in the same program. This was the first time I gave any thought to how many people on the rez drank and thought they had it under control, just like I had. Clearly, we did not have control over substances as long as trauma still reigned in our DNA. Alcohol was our main method of silencing the pain. There were alcoholics, addicts, and even guys from prison in the treatment centre with us. I spent a lot of time journaling on my own. We would gather in the spiritual room for sharing circles and pass a feather once a day in a large group, then again in smaller groups in the middle of the day for reflection and more sharing. The anger, the pain, all the deaths, everything we each had lost, children in foster care—so much pain and trauma came draining out of us.

As a leader and role model in my home community, I recognized I had to change. Towards this end, I found that sharing chores, which recreated living communally, was a huge part of my healing journey. If we needed to talk, there was an elder there 24/7. We spent a day of silence during the program on a nearby beach. Twenty-five of us walked the beach, praying and contemplating our decision to stop drinking. I picked up a rock like I always do when I'm out walking. We had a sharing circle eight hours later to discuss how the day went for us. I showed the rock I had found and shared what it meant to me. It was a one-inch oval stone wrapped in a shell that was shaped like Mother Mary holding her palms up in front of her in prayer. Finding this stone meant a lot to me, as it held significant meaning for me. My prayers were answered.

This is where I first experienced the benefits of bathing in cold water as a spiritual practice. The ladies would go first, in groups of four, at 5 a.m. We wore shorts and T-shirts, along with a bathrobe, and walked out to a spiritual pond nestled in the backyard, surrounded by cedar trees. The pond had a little stairway into the water, and a skin of ice formed on top. Whoever went first won the privilege of breaking the ice. I held sacred tobacco in one hand and humbly offered prayers in all four directions. I prayed the ancestors would bless me with their presence and support me through this endeavour toward wellness and sobriety. I dunked under the water, first to the east, then south, then west, and finally to the north, with a different prayer for each direction. In the state of spiritual connection, I did not feel the coldness of the water, but only a sense of euphoria and connection to the universe and all living things. We did this each morning for four days in a row.

On the fourth day after the spiritual bath, I went to my room, exhilarated and drained. I crashed on my bunk bed, fully alert, closed my eyes, and rested on our 30-minute break. I drifted off to sleep with the subtle hum of people talking and laughing. It was then that my spirit left my body and drifted through the bunk bed above me. I reached out to grasp the bed, and my arm went right through it as I kept levitating. I remember feeling scared and wondering what the heck was happening to me. I sat on the bed next to me and watched myself sleep. Still scared and in awe, I turned the bedside lamp on and sat there for a bit. I got up and walked out of the bedroom. In the doorway, I turned and saw that my body was still sleeping on the bottom bunk. I carried on walking throughout the building, which was shaped like a square hallway that went around an outdoor garden area designated for smoking. I could see and hear what everyone else was doing in the gym, the kitchen, and the lounging area. I walked back to my room, went back into my body, and woke up wondering what had just happened. The light was not on. I sat there, still in awe.

Later, I asked my cousin and her friends if that had ever happened to them. They said, "You better go and talk to the elder and ask her about it." I wasn't quite sure how to feel about this—afraid, nervous, or excited!

I walked into the elder's lounging room down the hall and next to the main office and sat with Matilda, a 75-plus-year-old plump First Nations lady with short white permed hair. "What can I do for you?"

I offered her tobacco, which is a portal/protocol of Indigenous peoples for what I am asking to be answered through her wisdom as a knowledge-keeper. I explained what had happened to me after the four days of spiritual bathing. She wasn't sure what I was talking about. Apparently, it is rare to astro-travel. I remember my late uncle/spiritual leader at home telling me about this happening to him and how he honed it. He was eventually able to astro-travel to ceremonies in the Dakotas while in his home sweat lodge. When he was summoned to go, he would go. He also talked about dream travel to other planets and the clouds.

The elder suggested I request a burning to feed the ancestors. I wasn't sure what she meant. I took her wisdom back to my cousin, who explained to me about the coastal and Squamish Nation ways of burning traditional food to feed the ancestors. My ancestors are my late grandma, aunties, one brother, uncles, and cousins from two generations back. It is believed that when we feed their spirits, they keep helping us and supporting us in continuing to strive to be *uxwalmixc* (people of the land). Call your spirit back, they say. Alcohol and drugs have a spirit that takes us over when we become addicted, so we must call our spirits back, *sima wi yiktsa7* (come here, Yiktsa7, Carol). We say it four times. I wasn't quite sure when and where that would happen. How do I request that such a spiritual event happen for me? I had never experienced such a cultural and traditional ceremony before. Who am I to be summoned by the ancestors to do these things that I never understood?

At four weeks, on our first-weekend pass, my cousin and I booked a hotel room, then spent a night pubbing and drinking non-alcoholic beer, thinking that it was okay while we wished to have a real beer or gin and tonic. A Peruvian guy in the treatment program was interested in me and asked me to drive up the island. I went along. It was fun driving in the rain in a 1967 convertible, flirting, and feeling brand new again. When we got back to the treatment facility about an hour after our curfew, the head counsellor met us in the parking lot. "You're late. You have to leave the program." Kicked out without any notice. They had someone gather our stuff; I caught a ferry back to the mainland. But I still believe we should have had a chance to explain to the group that we didn't start a relationship while in the program. I now understand. Two weeks from completion, I sabotaged my wellness treatment because I was afraid of the spiritual power that came with sobriety.

Being made wrong and at fault with no chance for explanation opened old wounds and memories of family trauma and the intergenerational impacts of the residential schools my parents and grandparents were made to attend. Every death in my family was a result of alcoholism. My Papa, in 1975, when drinking, committed suicide by running a hose from the exhaust into the interior of his red pickup truck. My oldest brother, only 15 at the time, was the one to discover our papa. Traumatized, he drank himself to death by the age of 32. In 1985, my auntie was killed in a car crash. My brother was driving home from the local June 4X4 rally; they were all drunk. My cousin, who passed out on the local festival grounds, was run over by a drunk driver in 1993. One after another, my family members were dying; there was no relief from the pain and grief—only the alcohol to attempt to numb it all.

After being kicked out of the drug and alcohol treatment centre, I managed sobriety for seven years by realizing I had to heal from the residential school syndrome. In my mind and heart, all the deaths link back to our parents and grandparents losing the right to raise their children in traditional *uxwalmixc* ways of life. I didn't want my children to wake up to drunks on the floor anymore. I wanted them to grow up to be more than I could ever be.

My brother invited me to attend Breath Integration Therapy workshops with him, where I could learn to breathe consciously in a regulated environment, allowing old mental and emotional wounds stuck in my body to be released through the breath. Together, we took the first training in Kamloops, where we started our healing journey together. I remember curling up on the floor in the fetal position, crying like a newborn baby, releasing all that trauma and all that pain that stemmed from the intergenerational impacts of residential school—pounding and kicking that energy out of me. I realized what I was holding onto was not only my own trauma but also that of my auntie, who died in '85; my brother, who was fed alcohol as a little boy; and my cousin, who was forced to attend residential school. I cried all weekend.

Rising above the trauma with the breathwork, we landed in a strange euphoric state, laughing and crying, and held one another's space through those moments. We came through the other side feeling lighter, refreshed, and clearer on our healing journeys. I didn't realize just how much I held my breath—every time I was yelled at, raped, forced to drink alcohol, or when fear stopped me in my tracks. After the weekend, I was able to go back home and run the family restaurant business for four years, where I succumbed to workaholism.

In the spring of 1998—burnt-out—my body demanded a break. I fell into what I now know was a spiritual sickness or an awakening. It brought me back to the time when my spirit left my body while I was at the treatment center. I believe it was due to neglecting the healing process. I drowned myself in work and didn't take time to keep up the breathwork. I ignored my body's signs telling me to rest and heal. There is still more to do. I fell sick; an energy came over me while cooking and putting an order together. When cashing out their order at the till, I froze. I didn't know what to do. Stupefied, I stood there in shock, looking at the customer, unable to complete a task I had done multiple times a day for the past four years.

I went home. The next day, I fell into a fever with cold chills. I stayed in bed, not able to warm up or cool down. I couldn't eat anything; I only drank water and ate a cracker. I lay in bed dreaming that I was a little black bear talking to my papa and mama, also bears. We were in their old house, where my grandmother raised my dad and his siblings in the '40s. I ran, played, and crawled under the house; we ate together, laughed, and talked all while being bears.

Like Goldilocks, I felt free and painless while in *dreamtime*. This went on for about three weeks. In and out of the hospital emergency room, the doctors had no idea what was going on with me. My irregular heartbeat felt like it had an extra heartbeat pounding out of my chest. My white blood platelet count was down. Four days in a row, they had to put me on an IV for dehydration for a few hours, then sent me home again. Next, my eyes were so light-sensitive that I could not open them. I stayed and slept in a dark room with my head covered, and protected my eyes with dark sunglasses whenever I left the room to go to the bathroom or kitchen. My eyes carried on like this for two weeks. The kids and their father looked after me the whole time. Cold sweats and chills continued from the beginning, requiring me to change my bedding almost daily.

I vividly recall the day when my father was repairing his skidder outside of our house, and a little black bear kept circling around. Like I used to do as a child, playing around his machinery and crawling underneath with him, asking, "What's this? What's that for?" Tiring of this bear, he took his gun from the cab, aimed, and shot. The bear ran towards the river. Dad asked his cousin to track it for the claws and fur. Albert couldn't find the bear or a blood trail. Dad was shocked because the bullet had found its mark. In my dream, I remember being so weak but wanting to go out to see what he was shooting at. AS me, the child, IN my dream, I WAS that spirit bear healing and recapturing my childhood innocence and that of my ancestors (bears), as I tossed and turned in bed in the present day. My spirit bears continued to stay close as I healed through this sickness.

After eight weeks of being sick, I pleaded with the Creator to hear my prayer, take me now, good Creator, or show me why I am going through this pain I didn't want to feel anymore! I lay there in the middle of my bed, sweating and cold. A white light, six inches round, emerged from the east corner of the bedroom ceiling. The light hovered above me for about a minute and went into my belly button, pushing me into the mattress. It then shot down my right leg, which went flying to the right corner of the bed; the light came up to my belly button again and shot down the left leg, then my right arm and my left arm. It felt like I was being exorcised or resurrected; I wasn't sure which… I must have been screaming because my son's dad came running into the room shouting, "Are you okay? Are you okay?" I lay there, knowing I was going to get well. I could breathe again;

the sweats and the chills left me! I cried so hard in relief and kept saying in shock, "I'm not sick anymore."

I began eating burdock, plantain, and dandelion roots to help build up strength in my liver, kidneys, and stomach, which took a beating through that illness. I ate wild rice. I drank organ grape root and devil's club tea to help my body regain strength and balance. Little did I know that I became what I ate. Filling my body with purity and earthly love a little bit at a time. I had no idea what the creator was preparing me for. I became the roots; they became me. One early morning, I couldn't get used to the father of my boys returning to our bed. I moved to the couch and fell back into a deep sleep. The boy's dad came and lifted the blankets off me, asking me why I had moved to the couch. As he lifted the blankets, I felt like a bed of roots being torn from the earth, torn away from deep love and comfort—my connection to the land that had consumed me since eating only earth food. I gasped for air and wailed.

Sleeping alone felt like every toxic thing in my life I encountered was gone. I was thinking, feeling, and knowing things more clearly. Mentally, physically, spiritually, and emotionally, I felt more balanced and open to all living things. The love and light in me saw the love and light in everything around me. The balance was so profound, but I had no one to turn to who understood what it all meant. This was the beginning of cleansing, both known and unknown. All the toxicity had kept me and my children from wholeness and holiness.

I built a sweat lodge for myself and my 11-year-old daughter. It opened my heart and soul, allowing her to open hers. It built our relationship. We connected to the creator together. We sat in the lodge with the embers of the glowing grandfathers (lava rocks). We prayed together, cried together, and pleaded for a better life together. We sang our *uxwalmixc* songs and invited our ancestors and spirit guides to hear our hearts of gratitude. We came to the mutual conclusion that all toxicity had to be removed from our lives. We humbled ourselves to our Indigenous sacred ways that our souls yearned for... beginning a journey there was no turning back from. Continuing to grow together, we solidified our relationship even further in her thirteen-moon womanhood ceremony. In that traditional circle of women, I understood I had to separate from my boys' father. It was time for me to be there solely for my children.

What I experienced was my superpower, which I am only beginning to understand. Being led by spirit is my cultural duty. Needing to understand more, I began a First Nations Women's Studies program. With encouragement from a traditional healer, who had helped my family through troubling times, I entered the Holistic Health Practitioner degree program. This was a path where I could share my ancestral knowledge to help others weave what they needed into their own lives and bring themselves to their highest good.

I learned how to make traditional medicines and gather traditional foods off the land from my late grandmother, mother-in-law, and uncles. I began Tse'lacha Wellness Healing Arts to share traditional medicines and integrate traditional healing practices into what I learned from Reiki, Shiatsu, lymphatic drainage massage, aromatherapy, and Breath Integration. I am an avid basket weaver of cedar bark and cedar root, creating workshops to connect people to the land and our way of life. Through these activities, I call myself and others back to our roots. Today, I lead sweat lodge ceremonies with my children and grandchildren. There, I teach them about what I have learned on my journey in hopes that we continue to walk our land and bathe in our rivers together—to create a better life for my great-grandchildren and great-great-grandchildren to come. All my relations...

www.facebook.com/tselacha

Guerrilla Grands

by Alma Lee Byzewski

Guerre, Guerra, Guerilla; words for war and the soldiers who fight the war. The word "Guerre" holds a nuanced meaning in the seemingly endless human condition of war. It is often the descriptor for a more minor war, "a war within a war," associated mostly with civil wars. Insidious by nature, a *Guerra-war* brings countries to their knees by destroying family ties, breaking established bonds, and nullifying loving connections.

Guerrilla warriors are often regarded as freedom fighters, soldiers bound to a noble cause, seemingly doomed to failure, minimized, and mocked for their ideals.

Throughout history, the identities of some guerilla leaders have become known. They are hailed as heroes, while the soldiers remain anonymous. Their importance is unquestionable and undeniable—the invisible citizen heroes who are simply acknowledged collectively: The French Resistance, the Polish Partisans, and the Underground Railroad were nameless people bravely doing the work, engaged and dedicated, challenging oppression, and giving value to life by risking their own lives.

The great freedom fighters of our time, Martin Luther King and Nelson Mandela, led movements based on hope, and what that hope generated was freedom—a grand hope for something better, kinder, more just, and more equal. Guerrilla fighters of hope: the former symbolically crossed a bridge; the latter called his jailers "friends." They showed us the possibilities—that our small wars for fairness and life can be won. One guerrilla fighter is capable of saving a life.

I know this because I am a guerrilla fighter.

I embrace the role, even with all the dubious connotations. Out of practical necessity, a guerrilla fighter operates secretly, uses improvised methods, learns surveillance techniques, and answers no questions.

I have been in the underground for over a decade, fighting to keep my cherished child alive and fighting for the beloved child of my child. The fight springs from the heart, is fought with conviction, and is fought for people unable to fight for themselves.

Something a guerrilla fighter knows with certainty: "The end does justify the means."

I am not a volunteer guerrilla fighter.

I am a conscript, rudely drafted by unimaginable circumstances and disciplined by fear. I arrived unarmed, untrained, disoriented, and desperate, and like the others in the fight, I wore a thick armour of tears and scarred heart tissue and looked at the world through tired eyes that could no longer cry.

I began to notice other grandparents.

I recognized the others by their eyes. Tired but alert, eyes that have seen too much. Eyes that never close—lest they miss a glimpse of their missing children. Eyes trained on the children of their children are sharp and cautious. We all know the stakes in this war.

The Grandparents are always present, always on duty, blending into the background colours, camouflaged, a uniquely equipped squad of caregivers. An underground of grandparents, deliberately staying invisible, the grandparents are a formidable front in the epidemic battles of daily drug deaths. Stepping up to nurture little lives simultaneously in the fight for the lives of their own adult children, knowing our lost children are also the parents of the next generation, of the future.

A disconnection so profound that a single drug deal maims three generations. When it is too late, when the *Guerra* claims another life, either by death or irrevocable damage, by jail and no contact orders, it is the Grandparents who step in to shelter the abandoned, neglected, orphaned children of the opioid epidemic.

Guerrilla Fighters, the Grands, some caring for many children—these grandparents are pivotal in keeping family ties strong; they are the instruments of love, stability, and protection. Guerrilla Grands command the power to win the "war within a war" through knowledge, wisdom, and fearlessness in the fight. Grandparents have unique skills forged by life. We have practical skills, a lifetime of professional contacts, valuable friendships, and knowledge of the "how" to achieve results.

Guerrilla Grands are the elite troops of the *Guerre*. Other fighters look to the Grands for advice, direction, support, and triage.

When a Guerrilla Grand decides to speak publicly, others listen. They hear our desire to shield grandchildren and to give them as much of a happy childhood as possible as our unwritten principle. This code is respected. The children of our children, ancient bonds spoken of biblically. "The children of your children are your crowns." (Proverbs 17:6.)

Guerrilla Grands don different robes, practice many roles, and are interchangeable to match unexpected moments, our crowns cradled firm and safe within our arms. Mostly, Guerrilla Grands, like all guerrilla fighters, remain quiet and solidly devoted. They replace retirement vacations with bus schedules, homework assignments, and dental appointments.

I am hopeful for the future, keeping love as the Grands' guerrilla weapon of choice.

As a parent and mother, I never doubted my children would thrive, be happy, and grow into productive members of Canadian society. They had the luxury of choice—to become, to do, to follow their dreams. Love, stability, and education are all guaranteed and given generously. One child played hockey for eleven years; the other was an equestrian with a beautiful quarter horse, the pair decorated with countless ribbons. They did well at school; they had many friends. As a family, we spent summers together at a beautiful lake.

Idyllic holidays swimming, boating, fishing, campfires, and visiting relatives. Until it wasn't.

Tragically, my husband suffered a massive stroke during heart surgery. The father my daughter adored disappeared, only to reappear as a brain-damaged stranger without the ability to speak. Within months, my son graduated from college and left to accept his first professional position as a flight paramedic up north, far away. In what felt like minutes, my little family dissolved.

My daughter, still in high school, turned to some of her friends for support—the ones who partied. She turned first to alcohol; she had already been smoking weed, and then the pills followed in an attempt to fill in the empty spaces and dull the grief.

A full slide into harder drugs was a poor, vicious, deceiving imitation of all that was lost.

She did not graduate from high school. The math teacher called, distressed that his best student had not written the final exam. He offered up another chance that was never taken. Such destructive patterns derailed her future.

Strange, unfamiliar friends replaced old childhood friends. Alcohol and drugs were everywhere and in control of my daughter. Her vehicle was impounded, driven by a drunk friend trying to elude the police.

The court summons began arriving. Speeding, reckless driving, and others more ominous would follow. No sense or reason reached her. She became more and more reckless and disconnected. Every day brought more ugliness into my life. We fought constantly over money; she was always in need of larger amounts, always in a hurry, rushing, and frantic to leave. She was incapable of caring, and out of complete ignorance, I was incapable of recognizing the danger my daughter was in. I was unaware that a disease was metastasizing before my eyes.

My daughter lost job after job and grew sicker by the day until one day; she did not return home. Days passed without any contact. Her cell was turned off; even after the 100th try, I called frantically, compulsively.

The empty sound of disconnection would be the background noise for years.

One night, she told me that only her new friends loved and understood her. It was the first time I would hear the drug talk that would keep her trapped and hold her hostage, the first glimpse of the brainwashing of a deadly cult—the breaking of family ties and the forced isolation and estrangement. The first tool of control and manipulation would be reinforced in many versions over the next year. Slowly, she was convinced I was the enemy. I could not be trusted. It made it easier for her to steal from me and abuse me. Her "loving friends" provided the drugs. She provided rent money, items to pawn, a perfect place to stash drugs, and even a handgun, all at the expense of her childhood home, turning me into a target of exploitation. My shed, my husband's retreat, was drafted to hide stolen goods like a stroller. Two strange, aggressive men trespassed. "We are here to pick up the stuff. Where is it?" Pushing past me, they took several items, but their primary interest was the stroller. What they were really after was the handgun hidden in the innocent device.

This was the turning point. I realized I was cynically co-opted, made part of a sick circle, as callously misused as my daughter, who in turn abused me, all in service of keeping her friends happy and guaranteeing their supply of drug money.

At this point, I viewed my daughter's companions as worthless, pathetic junkies, thieves, liars, and criminals. I hated them. I wanted to be their *Angel of Death*. My daughter's darkness was transferred to me by some wicked osmosis. I was no longer able to deflect the darkness.

When she did return, she would be belligerent and increasingly violent, physically attacking me for money and my phone, loading up her backpack with groceries, heaping verbal insults, and dissolving into tears. Sometimes, she would fall asleep on the couch. She was so young and vulnerable that it tore me apart inside even to look at my child and feel utterly helpless.

Always, I hoped she would stay, wake up, and ask for help. Invariably, when she left, some vehicle waiting around the corner would speed away. More and more, I feared I would never see her again. Increasingly, she appeared bruised, with purple around one eye and a hand that was swollen red and hot to the touch; she was dirty, wearing odd clothes, and sores appeared on her face and her legs. Her mouth hurt, all the orthodontics of her beautiful smile being eroded. I became as frantic as she was, begging her to stay, even for one night. I always told her I loved her, fearing those words would be my final words to my only daughter. Mostly, I talked to her back as she fled, running away from memories.

The shadows lengthened, drowning out all light, and the great desire to smash heads began to grow. I knew I needed to save myself. I knew I needed to save my daughter. I knew I needed new tactics. I could no longer avoid the trenches of this warfare encroaching ever closer. I felt a Guerrilla Fighter waking up, ready to rise.

She was malnourished and very sick; needles had delivered hepatitis C. There were open abscesses on her arms, scarred from injections of the drugs. She thought she was pregnant. She was no longer useful to her *friends*. With my home as her last resort; she returned.

A Guerrilla Mother took over, rising out of the ashes, knowing this was her last chance at life. I would do anything to thwart death. I felt the power of a Guerrilla Mother, feverish but focused. Suddenly, a small flame of hope flickered—a vague hope for the future.

Hope is a feathered thing, an indestructible Phoenix, ash-covered, singing a tune; the words you supply are yours forged from fire.

I also know guerrilla fighters appear in many forms. Our family doctor stayed past 9 p.m. after she examined my daughter, making many calls and asking colleagues to make exceptions, calling in professional favours.

Other fighters and medical specialists managed to bring a tiny, very early baby into the world in the liminal light of January. As I drove home, my car cited the temperature as 50 below. "How is this possible?"

For the first time in years, I took a moment to thank God for "tender mercies."

My daughter worked hard to regain her health, work at recovery, and be a good mother. It was not easy. The baby needed to remain in the NICU for three weeks. Born addicted, a little soldier, the newest fighter in an old battle.

They were discharged into my care and returned to my home only after an interdisciplinary meeting with every agency at the table. Later, I realized that my grandchild had barely escaped foster care, had been under a birth watch, and might very easily have been taken away by strangers to be placed with other strangers. Guerrilla Grandmother burned hotter than ever; combustible parts were gradually replaced with steel. Steel that would be tempered in a blast furnace of relapse.

The call came to meet the police at the ER. My daughter, drugged, beaten, and close to death, had been dumped at the ER doors.

Her partner was arrested and guarded by Police in the ER; in a drug-induced psychosis, he continued spreading mayhem.

I met the Special Constable for Intimate Partner Violence. She shrugged with dismissive indifference, "Maybe charges will be laid."

From the mouth of Guerrilla Mother/Grandmother, I inform the Special Constable of what charges will be laid. I give her the criminal codes. I speak Guerilla, "Do your job now, or you won't have one by tomorrow." Unaware of other patients nearby, unaware of how the security guards rose from their stools, then circled me, ready to back up this lone Special Constable. As if she were defenseless, geared up with her vest, her gun… The unscripted applause that followed my edict told every adrenalized cell vibrating in my body that I was justified in my words.

It was a pivotal moment, joyless and frightening.

All the horrible possibilities crowded around me.

With unshakable certainty, I knew my daughter's baby needed protection. From violence, from a compromised and fragile mother, and from exposure to deadly drugs.

I would be the protector, Guerrilla Grandmother, heart and soul. In true guerrilla fashion, I began by building an arsenal—strange weapons. I adopted a rescue dog, young, with wary eyes, on alert. I recycled Christmas bells and hung them on the gates and my doors.

I spread gravel, the pretty white kind, along the walkways; the crunch of the little stones was unmistakable to the canine ear. I did not answer my door to strangers.

My home turned into a fortress for the protection of an innocent baby. A Guerrilla Grandmother and her guard dog on duty are serious and possibly dangerous.

I began a litany of calls: Protection Orders, No Contact, and No Trespassing.

My address is on a list for quick response and victim witness protection.

I call Social Services, sign papers, open a file, am assigned a social worker, and am notified of court dates.

I speak to doctors, psychiatrists, and mental health nurses. I look up treatment centres. I speak to my daughter. Finally, she is ready to try to regain her health, seek treatment, and stay alive for her child. She sounds like someone I used to know. I try to remain pragmatic and realistic.

Simultaneously, I make my own plans. I make my own lists. I pulled my pension five years early. I put my business on hold. I am a changed person. I settled in to occupy my office at Guerrilla Grand.

Once all disguises are peeled away, the enemy is revealed in its most basic, elemental form: Death.

Everything else is a detail. It is also startlingly clear that Death's minions are everywhere. The drug trade—the distributors, the dealers, the pushers, and the willing hosts. There's also the indifference of elected officials, the ideologues who promote ignorance and hate, all in a bid to score votes. Death reaps its victims: greedy, unchallenged.

The "wars within the war" are fought increasingly by regular citizens. Demands are made to find a remedy for people experiencing homelessness and to fund street outreach. Ordinary people are requesting funds, showing up at meetings, and using their voices, determined to find a solution. They are recruits, a new version of Guerrilla Fighters.

Addictions and substance misuse are slowly being renamed and gently but persuasively sheltered under a healthcare umbrella. Still tenuous, controversial, and challenged, new forms of help are emerging. The messages from Guerrilla Fighters are being decoded, understood, and cautiously implemented.

Meanwhile, the Guerrilla Grands remain on duty. Hopeful of breakthroughs, kinder politics, and sane and fully funded programs, we remain steadfast, still doing the hand-to-heart work that wins wars, defies the odds, and upholds ideals—the work of love.

We are the Guerrilla Grands.

Chasing Symptoms

by Brenda-Lynn Haley

In November of 2006, they found him shirtless, no ID, dead, face down in a pile of vomit at the Granville Hotel in Vancouver, B.C. It took the Royal Canadian Mounted Police three weeks to identify the body and locate his next of kin. He had been living there since the '70s, as it was the warmest place to live in Canada at that time.

Living as a street person or couch-surfing most of his life due to drug and alcohol addiction, he spent years trying to overcome the trauma of childhood abuse and neglect.

His mother abandoned him and his five siblings, along with their alcoholic father, just before he turned three. On his third birthday, he was dropped off at an orphanage in a small town in rural Quebec, along with his two youngest sisters. Their dad just couldn't take care of them, and neither could his older siblings. That boy—Billy—was destined to become my biological father.

In 1969, my mother spotted him wearing his army uniform, shielding from the cold in the archway of Rosberg's building in Niagara Falls, smoking a cigarette. She thought he was so handsome with his piercing blue eyes and pouty lips. She told me years later that he had nowhere to live, so she paid for him to stay in a hotel and took him food daily from the restaurant where she worked as a hostess.

I was born ten months later. However, while she was pregnant with me, she and Billy and his friends went to the beach. It was here that she saw him drinking, doing drugs and instigating trouble. It was then that she decided she didn't want her baby to grow up surrounded by that kind of behaviour.

She broke up with him, never allowing him to see me without supervision. By the time I turned two, she was not allowing him to see me at all, as he always showed up drunk looking for a fight.

I don't know the whole story, as my mom has passed away. But I do know that my life was not saved from the heavy burden of addiction, as I grew up with a stepfather who was also an alcoholic.

On the other hand, I was loved and adored by my parents, but it was not without my own struggles. I grew up with medical trauma.

I was gifted a dislocated hip at birth, as was my paternal uncle. Congenital dislocation of the hip runs in that side of the family. I had two hip surgeries during the first six years of my life. When I turned one and started walking, I began falling more than the average toddler, alarming my mother. That's when the doctors discovered my hip issue. I was then placed in traction with my legs casted from waist to ankles to correct the hip. I have no idea how my poor mother carried me around on her hip all that time. My legs were set in plaster, spreading them apart.

My grandfather, a skilled carpenter, made me a custom-fit highchair to accommodate the cast, which spread my legs out to four feet wide. Now my mother could lift the food tray sideways, plunk me in, and fold the tray down. Then I could sit on my own without support and be as normal a toddler as possible.

That surgery worked until I was six years old. Then I needed a full bone graft. In 1975, a cutting-edge operation had the orthopaedic surgeon take a chunk of my upper pelvic bone and graft it to the top of my femoral joint, as mine was just not big enough, which allowed the head of my hipbone to stay in the socket.

However, this time it wasn't just my legs that were placed in plaster. I was put in a full-body cast, from my armpits to the tips of my toes. At the age of six, I was growing fast, and I remember the doctor having to cut a square hole in the stomach of the cast, so that I could breathe properly. I also had to have a schoolteacher, Mrs. Smart, come every weekday after school to teach me how to read and write so that I wouldn't fall behind in school. I remember crying and begging to be out of that cast so I could run, skip, and play with my friends instead of watching from the hospital bed in front of our living room bay window. I don't know what was more isolating—watching from my bed inside or when my strong dad carried me with all that heavy plaster sideways through the door to a borrowed lounger and watching them play up close.

Possibly worse, the doctors followed up that body cast with a walking cast that made me walk like a disabled duck. It hurt. A lot. When I would ask the nurses if I could stop walking the parallel bars, I'd be told, "Quit your whining and just do it."

When they changed the dressings, they found the pressure of being mobile had caused a blood clot. I begged, "Can we please wait for my mother?" No dice. I was alone and at their mercy.

Looking back now, I wonder just how much medication my poor mother had to give me in order to keep me sedated enough and free from the pain from the pins that were fusing my bones together. How else could you keep a six-year-old calm? When I was in kindergarten, they even had to pull my four front teeth, as they were rotten from all of the medication needed to keep me somewhat free of pain.

During the next 36 years, my hip supported me in my career, active sports, and social life. However, in December of 2011, I took a medical leave from my job as an Early Childhood Resource Teacher and waited for a hip replacement. My hip joint was now splinters and shards of bone shifting and clicking with every move I made. Every step I took caused excruciating pain, even more so when the hip froze me in place and I had to break free. People could hear the crack of the bone popping loose. The pain became so intense that I could no longer manage it with regular acetaminophen. Nothing was helping.

It was then that my doctor prescribed me pain medication. The compound ingredients were tramadol (a form of opium) and acetaminophen. This quick-acting pill was a life-saver for me.

At least for a few years.

I didn't want to take anything addictive, as I knew I had a predisposition to addictive behaviour given the history of my biological father and growing up with my dad, who raised me. However, the doctor reassured me that it was the least addictive out of the myriad of opioids that were available. I was desperate to escape the intense pain. I trusted his judgment.

When I was 16, I recall taking acetaminophen with codeine for monthly migraines and for my hip pain from my days of figure skating. It was such a relief to have a temporary release from the pain and catch a few moments of euphoria. I don't have any memory of my life ever being without some form of pain in my hip.

In 2016, I was in a car accident, injuring my lower back, sciatica, and right shoulder. I was also diagnosed at that time with fibromyalgia.

The need to continue with this diet of pills morphed into daily rituals of taking up to eight tramadol pills a day, two at a time. This abuse started causing havoc on my stomach, and the doctors just piled more drugs on me. (ziprasidone, cylcobenzaprine, pantoprazole, buspar, lamictal, lorazepam, pregabalin, and zopiclone.)

In February 2023, I realized just how much I was depending on my tramadol to get through the day. If I didn't take it, my pain would be unbearable, and my energy levels would plummet. Taking tramadol was how I got through a Dominican trip with friends. Disembarking from our flight, I remember my friend's husband saying, "Hey Brenny, try not to take any more pills today when you get home."

My first thought was very defensive, *You have no idea how much pain I'm in.*

Then it hit me.

I AM AN ADDICT!

When I got home, I started to research the side effects of long-term use of tramadol. The main one is rebound pain. When the drugs start to drop off, the pain becomes very intense—at least mine was—all over my arms, legs, and joints.

That's when I started to pay attention to the pain and the medications I was taking. I understand now that I never had the chance to develop my own independent thinking and just always trusted my doctors. *Listen to your doctor; they know best.*

Don't get me wrong, I'm very grateful that I have a family doctor, but he's only one person with thousands of patients.

I then took matters into my own hands and decided that I would start altering my medications. Well, that put me in a huge downward spiral. I ended up on the Mental Health and Addictions ward—in full blown psychosis. *(Note to reader: never go off meds without consulting your doctor and pharmacist.)* The hospital staff took one look at all of the drugs I was on: mammoth white pills, little white pills, blue oval pills, blue and white pills, large yellow pills, and round beige pills... they said they didn't have a clue how to modify all the pharmaceuticals that landed me in their ward.

During the next ten days, all of my mental health meds were changed, but I was still taking tramadol. A month after I got out of the hospital, I began a conversation with my pharmacist to slowly wean off the circus of tramadol. It took immense strength, courage, and determination. I was agitated and on edge for weeks, but that eventually subsided. I probably should have gone to rehab, but I didn't want to leave my family again. The ten days I spent in the hospital were more than enough for me.

I now feel free. Free from the tyrannical world of self-medicating and dependence on two yellow pills times four to get me through my days.

I'll never be totally free; as I know with addiction, it could be so easy just to fall into taking them again.

I still have pain, but I treat it by using my hot tub daily. I mind my diet and try to stay away from any inflammatory-causing foods, such as gluten, potatoes, tomatoes, and peppers. Massage therapy and gentle Hatha Yoga help to flush toxins, keep me grounded in the earth, and leave me feeling whole and heart-centred. The biggest godsend for me has been guided meditation and mindfulness-based stress reduction. This proven method is used worldwide. The breathwork, visualizations, loving-kindness mantras, and mental body scans allow me to stay present in the moment. Focusing on the positives alleviates stress, anxiety, depression, and, best of all, chronic pain. I have even taken to writing my own meditations, which has brought me great comfort.

I also did not get through this totally alone. When I confessed that I felt I was addicted to my tramadol and needed to stop taking them before they killed me, my partner, my children, and my best friends rose up around me and supported me. They say it takes a village to raise a child, but I also believe it takes a village to support an addict, and I'm so grateful to my family and friends for their unconditional love and support.

Looking back now, I realize it has been a lifelong dependency.

I no longer start my day with popping pills. This time last year, I was taking approximately 20 pills a day, just to get by. I would wake up in the morning in excruciating pain all over my body and take two tramadol. Even then, I had to sit in my shed, drink my tea and wait the half hour it took for the pills to kick in. My poor organs had to manage all those meds, especially my liver. I did the math. Over a 12-year period, I took approximately 35,000—yes, thirty-five thousand pills, just of the tramadol alone.

I recall looking at my reflection in the mirror and feeling like such a fraud—how the pills left me feeling so depleted. My soul was empty like a blown-out pysanky egg, ready to crack any minute. Even my bones felt hollow, full of air like an aerated chocolate bar. Full of pain and agitation, I was so tired of taking pills. It seemed like it was all I did. Feeling guilty and full of shame for how dependent I had become on these demons, I took matters into my own hands and took full charge of my life.

I still fight the demons every single day.

However, now my routine is different. I have turned to writing for my solace. It helps me by journaling all the reasons I'm grateful. When I start my day with a grateful heart, it keeps me in flow with a positive state of mind. I will probably fight this addiction for the rest of my life.

<u>My message that we can all benefit from:</u>

- Knowing our bodies.
- Doing our research.
- Paying attention to the symptoms and trying all forms of alternative medication before accepting any pain meds.

These are now my six non-negotiables, borrowed from my friend Michelle Hope-Wright:

Spelling the acronym DREAMS.

1. **Drink:** Drink lots of water to hydrate the body and the brain.
2. **Rewire:** Change your thought patterns through constant repetition.
3. **Exercise:** Move your body daily through gentle yoga, walking, and stretching.
4. **Antioxidants:** Fuel your cells on a molecular level.
5. **Mindfulness:** Practice daily mindfulness and meditation.
6. **Sleep:** Practice good sleep hygiene.

I have spent my entire life running from the pain. Numbing it physically and chasing it down with pills. I was crushing my emotions and trying to extinguish the physical symptoms temporarily, only to have to take more pills a few hours later.

It is too easy to be dragged under by pills, and then before you know it, you'll be on a psych ward like me, in rehab, or worse, dead like Billy.

There is such a huge stigma around opioid use and addiction. You really don't have to be down and out and homeless like my father to become an addict. I'm a professional and admit to being reluctant to share my experience. However, if my story helps just one person change the cycle of drug and alcohol addiction, then it has all been worth it. I know the merry-go-round of substance abuse. If it happened to me, it could happen to anyone.

I'm sharing this story because I know I'm not the only person going through life "Chasing Symptoms."

www.facebook.com/brenda.haley.125

Dark Castle

by Ben Goerner

Darkness. Midnight in a gothic castle hallway. Yet I still see shadows of the block on the walls, impenetrable, damp, and cold. I can smell the mould and decay in the air. I watch helplessly as the walls expand far away from me, as I remember from too many horror movies. Yet, inexplicably, the walls are also closing in on me at the same time—squeezing. The pressure on my chest is like someone sitting on me. I desperately try to capture the air with each gulp of breath. There's a hammer pounding inside my chest. A scream forms deep in my abdomen and vomits itself volcanically to the surface...

And then it's gone. Desolate, cold, and silent.

Small. Insignificant. Like nothing I will ever do will mean anything to anyone—except Tiny—that haunting presence within.

I see two bottles in front of me as I sit there, minuscule and futile in the chill of the darkness. The drops of condensation slide down the sides of each bottle in slow motion, like in the commercials during sports events on TV, dark yet strangely inviting and seductive. I feel an ominous longing.

The first drink is courage. It is full of vitality, potency, drive, satisfaction, and power. Oh, the sweet, sweet taste of fulfillment—of approval. The soothing taste of warmth, love, and acceptance trickles down my throat.

I spy the other bottle. It is passive, peaceful, yet impotent. It is an illusion, relaxation, manifest... It is contentment. It, too, feels like a warm hug as it trickles down my throat. It takes away the panic Tiny was feeling a moment ago. Medicine. It is a warm blanket, comfortably numb to everything around me, around Tiny.

They are the same bottle.

Tiny sits awkwardly, yet strangely comfortable, on the old Gothic castle's damp, hard stone floor. His back propped against the uneven, mouldy, damp stone. The room no longer moves or vibrates. The hammer is gone for us. All is at peace... for now.

The gothic midnight stone-cold castle with the walls simultaneously closing in and expanding was a dream I had as a child. It symbolized a feeling that followed me throughout my childhood and continued into adulthood. That feeling would invade my relationships and continually skulk in the shadows of my work.

That midnight feeling still exists now, its roots reaching deep into the unknown hidden crevices of my mind. It calls out to me occasionally, but I can't hear the words. I feel them. I don't understand, but I'm always left with an empty, insatiable desire for something. I don't know what.

And I wake up yelling and mumbling at the invisible presence that haunts me at the edge of my bed from time to time. Paralyzed, I search...

...for there is a place of light, solace, and sanctuary. And I can journey to that place as the light guides me through the darkness.

Words are the manifestation of my feelings, all of them, both dark and bright. They are my spirit speaking: strong, proud, humble, at peace, and in ready mode. They are the expression of my thoughts, sometimes clear as glass, sometimes like an ocean-side fog. Words are the blossoming of my spirit, which I see as the greater sum of all my parts. Writing words is often the healing move when things begin to close in and feel dark again. Words are often the candle in the window that leads me back home.

Music is like that too. It surrounds me like a warm blanket, or it puts me in a fighter jet cockpit. It breaks my heart or heals the wounds within. It gives me power and vitality, or peace and tranquillity. I sit at the piano, and my fingers come alive with emotion and meaning.

Similarly, playing my guitar is like caressing a lover for our mutual pleasure. The end of each piece is the story of love made, a challenge met, a victory earned, and a tear shed. Music is the perfect marriage between the spirit, the physical, the logical, and the mathematical.

Sometimes, I'll wake up in the middle of the night and write down the lyrics of a song that is constantly haunting me. I listen to the soothing waves of melody, like ocean waves on the shore. I feel the heartbeat of the bass and percussion, making my bones thrum with excitement. Yes, both peace and excitement can co-exist in a radical acceptance of the world and all that is.

At the same time, there's the power to change whatever it is that is streaming through my consciousness. I am satisfied. I am content.

For that is my writing and my music. An expression of all that is right, and all that is wrong in the world and inside of me.

This is what I desperately need—how I continue to heal—when I remember. When I'm not wound up in the chaos and minutiae of the world, when I'm not overwhelmed by the sorrow and screams of the past and present, these things help me crawl out of those midnight castle dungeons and leave me bathing in the sun's brilliance and warmth and the rain's cleansing wash: imagery, waves of vibration in music, and the magic of words.

The story of my healing is not a place. It is not somewhere I have arrived. Nor do I think I will ever do so. But it is a story of a journey through mountains and valleys, ocean currents, and streams that sometimes guide me and sometimes take me away from where I think I want to be. Overall, though, it is *my journey,* and though there may be undercurrents and valleys, there are also sanctuaries and rest stops along my path. There will always be different fruits I can choose to pick. Some will be succulent, yummy, and refreshing; some will be sour and make me gag. But they are all there as part of the creation I am aware of. They all have a secret to share with me. And it is this awareness that keeps me returning to the pathways that heal the scrapes, cuts, and bruises on my journey.

And so the music plays, the words flow, and the script commences.

I recall certain senses from my past. I remember the promising aromas of supper being prepared by my mother as she welcomed me home. Sometimes, even today, I imagine I can smell the sweetness of those decadently evil deserts she would create that would help us all forget, if only for a moment.

When I was young, in the late '60s, we had a gravel driveway even though we were in the big city. I would collapse at home, drained, and relieved that school was done for another day. While bathing in the luxurious aromas of my mom's baking, I would suddenly feel this chill climbing up my spine like a creeping, crawling spider. The rolling crunch of the gravel driveway signalled that my stepfather was arriving home from work. Even though that chill was just a couple of seconds, it would last for an eternity. A jolt of electricity would shoot through me like the shock of a farmer's electric fence as I heard the front door open and either click or bang closed. The sound dictated what I would do next.

I think I know when I began to be aware, at some level, of my trauma.

Suffice it to say, my stepfather and I had a problematic relationship from his introduction into the family when I was six years old through to my mid-20s. I had even left home at age 15 to escape the situation. But that is a chapter or two for another book, for another time.

He would arrive home from work, and the tension and anxiety would explode inside my head and all through my body—all spiders crawling and shocks! If I heard the bang, I would quickly slink away like our dog with his tail between his legs to my room. Sometimes, I would feel a cautious wave of relief when hearing just the click. I might not have to slither out of sight if that click signalled a "good" day for dear ol' dad.

Thankfully, not every day was bad, but there were enough bad days that would happen more randomly than expected. I know now that this unpredictability has reinforced my anxiety and tension. Eventually, there were spiders and shocks every day, regardless of the outcomes. The harbinger of that anxiety, even to this day, is the sound of rolling gravel and the sound of a door opening and closing—regardless of where I am or who I am with.

Breathe, awareness; I am mindful; I am not in the darkness of the castle. I am surrounded by white light.

Along with the anxiety that seemed to be increasing in my life, I was also becoming more distant. I was constantly in conflict with my stepfather. It seemed there was nothing I could do right. There was nowhere but my room where I could disappear. The constant belittling and exasperated, disgusted grunts from him when he would shove me out of the way made me feel like I was an annoying, unwanted pest.

Some may see this as a pity party, but the desolation of the emptiness I felt was and still is quite real at times. As I grew older, I realized this darkness would manifest in places of work and even in other close relationships. The anxiety would, and sometimes still does, leave me feeling useless and powerless.

Breathe, awareness; I am mindful; I am not in the darkness of the castle. I am surrounded by white light.

I can now see that I was feeling very betrayed as well as worthless and powerless. My safety was threatened, if not lost. I felt fear most of the time and rage the rest of it. I believe my fear and rage would mask and maybe even justify my depression and anxiety. I felt abandoned. I was isolated.

Trauma was festering inside of me, growing like rot and decay, from an annoying itch to a throbbing ache.

I needed something.

In that gothic old midnight castle, shrouded in fog and shade, Tiny and my demons hid and still hide. Moulded out of the mud from my childhood, they slither and creep. But as the poker hands got dealt out, they made their presence known more and more.

In the days of my youth, everyone and their dog smoked cigarettes. And most everyone in our circle drank alcohol. My mother was not so much into the drinking, but I noticed she was a smoking chimney for sure. We had a cabinet full of practically every type of alcohol you could imagine and more. Everything, everywhere, all the time in our house. We were a family of people trying to survive the formidable trials that life would dish out with the help of the alluring and temporary medicinal and mind-numbing, consoling combination of alcohol and nicotine—two of the most powerful drugs known to humankind.

As I grew, I noticed something. Whenever someone in my family was stressed or upset after an argument or after a difficult moment in the kitchen or in the garden, they would fire up a smoke. Smoking, I noticed, was a necessity amongst the adults, regardless of what was happening. Celebration, concentration, relaxation—there was always a dart hanging out of someone's mouth or burning a long tail of ash in the ashtray. The smoke in the house was as thick as a four-alarm fire at times, but I never noticed it, like most smokers.

And for some reason, I was forbidden to smoke! What was up with that? I was warned in no uncertain terms that I would be "beaten to a pulp" if I was ever caught smoking—my stepdad's feeble and eventually impotent attempt to threaten me yet again.

Enter the thrill, enter the challenge, enter the forbidden, enter the rebel yell, and enter the fuck you!

I was ten years old. I was at my aunt and uncle's farm, where everyone smoked. My uncle even showed me how he could roll a smoke with one hand while driving the farm truck with the other. I loved him. He was so cool and kind. Fatherly in many ways.

I don't remember where everyone was at the moment I started smoking. I saw my cousin's pack of smokes on the kitchen table, taunting me and daring me. I took one out, found a couple of matches (just in case), and when I had the chance, I went out back, hid behind a wall, and fired that bad boy up!

Redemption! Liberation! That warm hug! The middle finger! The ultimate Fuck You! And it felt and tasted like Tony-the-Tiger grrreat!

What I realized later in life is that I initiated the first of many addictive behaviours at that moment. I had committed a theft. I hid my intentions and my use, especially from my parents. I learned to hide, manipulate, and even lie from that one defining moment. I experienced the thrill of the forbidden risk and danger underneath. For the next four decades, smoking became my go-to anxiety reducer, celebration enhancer, personal validation tool, and personal power source—my escape from the dark castle. A magical vapour that all at once made me 10 feet tall. Even more so than other drugs I would soon discover. My life essentially revolved around cigarettes.

Breathe, awareness; I am mindful; I am not in the darkness of the castle. I am surrounded by white light.

Meanwhile, back to my youth. I discovered pot at age 12, booze at age 13, and hallucinogens at age 15. Once again, waves of joy and laughter were brought back into my life. I did not die or kill anyone with an axe, contrary to *Reefer Madness* (an anti-pot film from 1936) and the propaganda of the day. We were being lied to. Drugs were not harmful at all! They filled all my empty holes and lifted me up from Tiny to (almost) giant! I actually made more connections than I ever had before and enjoyed the parties and frivolity. After that, booze and drugs became necessary at any party. I did not feel like I fit or belonged, that I would be valuable or loved unless I was baked.

Eventually, though, I grew away from the "illegal" drugs. Alcohol and cigarettes remained a staple for decades and would be my go-to medication for stress and anxiety, though I would not realize that for years. They were my escape from the dark castle in my head to keep Tiny and his minions from harassing me.

I spent over thirty years as a counsellor, providing support for people struggling with addictions and homelessness. Alcohol followed me throughout my career. It was not problematic by definition for a long time, but slowly, it crept up on me as I travelled this road. I would even cut back or quit for years when I felt too out of control and enslaved. When drinking, I did not become violent or aggressive. When I indulged too much, people would tell me I was a happy drunk. I could belong, entertain, discuss shit I knew nothing about, and relate on the surface with people with whom I had little or nothing in common. I felt 10 feet tall, and I fit in… at least, that's what it felt like for a while.

But underneath, there was the darkness. Like in the castle, I felt like an outcast. Tiny. No one in those social circles wanted to hear the incredibly important stories about the struggles of those who were homeless. No one wanted to hear about the inequality that contributes to the ills of society and underlies the causes of mental health and substance use disorders. No one wanted to hear about the teen girl who told me how she was raped and beaten by the person that she trusted completely. Those conversations, if they ever happened, were the fun killers. If I ever brought up my world, I would feel like people would turn their heads away in fear and disgust.

So, I became the social imposter. I would drink, joke, and even play guitar to try to fit in. And I locked all of that other shit in the dark dungeons and growing cesspools of that gothic castle with the moving walls.

Eventually, in helping others, I began feeling powerless, overwhelmed, and ineffective. Alcohol crept up as an old coping friend. I had all of the traits of addiction from my smoking days. I quit smoking in 2006, but alcohol slowly stepped in as my new best friend. The one that would listen. The one that would keep me company in my quiet, safe solitude. The one that would help me forget the rape that little girl told me about. The guy whose dad beat him over the head with a two-by-four. The fellow who suffered from debilitating schizophrenia who thought he was going to have to kill me. All the women constantly victimized, raped, and beaten in vicious cycles of physical and sexual abuse who were driven to cope with the needle or the pipe and then banished from friends and family for doing so. Or the people graduating from a treatment program only to find no housing or other support. To find out there was no future despite their best efforts. Hopeless, powerless.

Then there were the others. The ones who constantly attacked and beat down those who were already suffering. The ones that drove by in their pickup trucks, swearing and throwing things at those who did not have homes or families—they were living out their worst nightmares in full view. When people videoed their plight and posted those videos on social media for all to see, what torment they must have felt. I felt for them. All of them. I longed for peace for those who suffered. The hopelessness I felt was a dark, ominous storm cloud, fully pregnant with destruction and hate. For three decades, I was swallowed up in the tsunami of grief and horror, with no light at the end of that castle hallway. The trauma I would embrace for them would almost destroy me.

The final straw? During the last five years of my work, before I crawled and clawed my way to my retirement, 50 people with whom I had worked extremely closely, perished from overdoses due to the poisoning of the illegal supply of drugs on the street. My job had become not unlike a M.A.S.H. unit in the wars. Triage. Reach for the survivors and treat the wounded. Stop at the side of the road on the way home from or on the way to work and get those fucking tears out in private. Isolate! Hide! Get Numb!

Near the end of that journey, alcohol did take over. It replaced my hope with numbness. That's what it was supposed to do. Give that warm, loving hug and that sense of peace. Comfortably numb.

As I write this, my emotions are on fire. The lump in my throat is oozing up like bile to the back of my mouth. I want to cry. I want to scream. Fuck you, world! You never gave a shit about these beautiful people! You could have cared less about them or their families. You wanted them to disappear! You never wanted them!

Fuck you, *Dad*! You could not have cared less about me. You were too busy. You were too lost in your own shit. You were too drunk. You were too stuck in your old-timey stagnation. You were so hurt by the war, all of your loss and grief, and you fucking passed it all to me!

I drank. And in the end, I drank to black out. Fuck it! I turned into the one who didn't care anymore, especially after I broke free from the hell of the war at work. The trauma that I had ignored in myself oozed back into my life. The door at the end of the castle's hallway slammed with a reverberating bang, eclipsing the light behind it. Tiny and those demons had arisen in full force.

I felt like such a failure—the imposter, the fake, the one who couldn't care for himself. But I didn't care.

Breathe, awareness; I am mindful; I am not in the darkness of the castle. I am surrounded by white light.

Until I did start caring again. Because, in the end, I know that's who I am. I do give a shit!

But not until I passed some of that hurt on to my own family. The shame and guilt were unendurable. But hope lived in forgiveness, not in a bottle. I am forever and profoundly grateful for that. Hope was the light in that dark castle. Hope for me and hope for those I love. A huge part of my healing has been to not only heal myself but to help the ones I love heal as well. And if nothing else, I was really good at doing that for others. It was—it is—my turn now.

But even now, as I hold back tears and squish down that lump in my throat to finish this story, I know that Tiny and The Demons (*sounds like a lame death metal band*) arose from my original trauma. I know that the demons in that lame death metal band led by Tiny are a metaphor. They are not real in any sense other than the triggers and reactions of the trauma I experienced as a child and then through my work. Nothing more than neural pathways—a rewiring, a re-programming, train tracks in my brain if you like—that could and are being replaced by different train tracks: healthier schemas, thoughts, and patterns. Real things that I could and can do something about.

My liberation:
Breathe, awareness; I am mindful;
I am surrounded by white light...

This is my mantra now. It is my prayer, meditation, and "trigger" for my health and healing. It is the lever that switches the direction of the train tracks, lighting up my new wiring. It brings me back to a place where a warm breeze blows on spring flowers in a meadow. It takes me to the ocean, where the waves lap or crash on the shore. It brings me to these words. It brings me to the music that constantly floats through my head, like a cool brook, or soars like a fighter jet. Peace. Action! My warm hug. What I have always and will always search for and embrace.

And for a moment, the sun disappears behind a dark cloud, with the promise of a storm. I forget. Because sometimes I do that, too.

And I forgive myself.

I remember when I see a dandelion break through the cement walkway. I remember how the sky breaks open with its deluge of cleansing wash or when it is full, clear blue, and endless. I remember when the mist floats through the forest to the ocean. I remember how words can heal as I write this. How being mindful and aware can heal, soothe, weaken, or even eradicate that tsunami. These words and my songs shine a light in the darkness of the castle. My music can vibrate into being and turn sadness into meaning and laughter into action.

Those pesky demons are mostly harmless now. But I must still be aware. And Tiny? Well, he still lurks in the shadows a bit. But I know how to deal with him. I accept and forgive him, for he is me in the past—cornered, scared, powerless—simply needing a genuine, warm hug.

www.domainoflife.ca

Pecking Order

by Helena Paivinen

"My name is Helena; I am an alcoholic and drug addict, amongst other things." I look around the room and at the eyes staring back at me.

"Hi Helena," people say in unison. I feel acknowledged, validated, recognized, and seen—something that everyone I believe wishes for in life, especially me, a junkie.

I am unlovable, damaged goods, dirty, and unclean. These beliefs have festered secretly inside for five decades, hidden from all, including me. Beliefs can be dangerous and more powerful than thoughts, as I hear them often cited as justifications behind religious killings and deaths.

I had no conscious awareness of these beliefs and the destruction they caused until years later, when I stopped to take an honest, close look at what had happened during decades of horrific substance abuse.

~

I'm little, and I sense that something is off, but I have no idea what. My family home is often silent—we sit down for three meals each day but rarely speak, except to thank Mom for the food afterwards.

Silence can scream.

I now think of that famous painting of the dark image screaming silently in a warped dimension. Apparently, the artist was depicting addiction.

Back in my childhood, I started school without knowing any English because we only spoke our native language, Finnish, at home. We Finns are known for being stoic and quiet. I cannot understand the strange sounds the other kids make when they seem to be speaking to me. I imagine them as chickens making cluck-clucking sounds. Chickens fit my experience, as these birds sense fear and tend to peck at strange, vulnerable, frail little ones.

They can be forgiven for mistaking me for an albino. I have rabbit-white eyelashes and white brows that reflect like flashlights in the sun. My eyes are not red but large, curious, and bright. Everything is foreign; I still can't make sense of the sounds the schoolchildren make. They group in small circles, kicking, scratching, and scraping dirt into the air.

Chickens sense and target small, vulnerable ones. The kids transform, become dangerous, and peck, peck, peck at me as I am tiny and frail. Drawing blood is fun for them. With razor-sharp claws, their beaks hurt as they tear out white feathers, disguised in my blonde hair.

Cluck, cluck, cluck, the children-chicks scrape, dirt flying about as they circle me. I am surrounded. I am the small, weird-to-them, vulnerable one. There is power in numbers; groupthink takes over, and mob mentality overtakes even the friendlier ones.

They hurl insults to hurt, projecting their own internal, unconscious pain. Children-chicks are vicious, violent, and mean.

A rooster appears; she is strong and fierce and understands the strange language I cannot speak. She is a Finlander like me. I am the target of her anger, which she cleverly and cruelly disguises as humour for other kids. She fluffs her feathers up and struts around me, scraping dirt into the air. Carrie is admired for her looks; she is the head chick, popular yet somewhat feared as others sense danger, panic, hurt, pain, and ruthlessness around her. She struts, roots, and rules the crowd. Feathers fluff and scatter about, which help soothe and appease her unconscious ruffled insides. I am surrounded now by her and all the others. They PECK, PECK, and PECK.

I am an outcast and need to stay hidden. Being invisible is the key.

At age 12, my family moved. I donned a solid, rigid cloak of fake confidence, pushing down, denying, and negating any internal feelings of anxiety, fear, or self-angst. To survive in this harsh, unyielding world, I had to make certain that I would no longer feel. I disconnected from all internal emotions and the powerful, intuitive energy within. I began to access, think, and rely only on my brain.

Thinking, not feeling, was key, as emotions—energy in motion—were too painful for me. Detachment was vital; I began to reside inside my head and exist only above my neck. My entire body below was dangerous ground, so my brain decided to protect me by taking complete charge.

Six years of closely observing and watching others had become life-preserving for me. During that time, my brain unconsciously learned and internalized how the bully-chickens faked being strong. From these long years of consistent daily data input, my brain commanded my mouth and body to mimic their strength—to stand rigidly tall and straighten up my spine to look stellar and strong!

My brain knew that popularity was vital to survival, so it dictated to my eyes to find the top chicken to befriend. Even though the other chickens were brutal and mean, my brain tells me a story: *That is not how I am. After all, I held little Jimmy's hand to protect him from being bullied.*

Little did I know the power of false stories—denial, some might say. My brain hides deep down, unconsciously inside, a reptilian protector that, when threatened, becomes powerfully reactive. Passed down through my parents, the invisible e-energy, an e-motion, moves through my being. Ancient ancestral genetics, the tiny DNA molecules of SISU, a Finnish word for strong spirit, arise within me.

Phoenix-like now, I arise from dirt and ashes and spread my no longer frail chicken-white feathers, which now look like strong, eagle-black wings. Sharp, hidden, inner claws, a bone-breaking beak—unlike the others, I am an imposter amongst them. I hide myself not only from them but also from me.

This was the first stage of the addictive disorder—to become disconnected from me. I learned that knowledge was key from my first six years in school. It seemed that kids with good grades were noticed. Rewards—gold-pasted stars and big-red checkmarks—were awarded when things were correct.

Being smart, having straight A's, and having great performances were where I needed to be! Off I went, entering straight into my head and cutting off my body to protect me from its exhausting emotional energy drain.

Throughout all these years, I have had constant, recurring SILENT SCEAM nightmares. I RUN from NAZI generals, hiding in ice-cold terror, motionless under dusty, dark beds. DO NOT breathe; small intakes—nasal air—vital for life—*DO NOT MOVE. BE STILL*, MY BRAIN COMMANDS MY BODY. I CAN NOT BREATHE. WHAT HAPPENED TO—Black-beetle shiny boots—right there—I'm filled with HORROR. Guns, dark murder, blood killings, violent death, rage-filled, scared SCREAMMMMMMSSSSS.

In this context of naive and rapid neuronal development, my regular use of substances began. At age fourteen, my brain discovered pot, the wonderful soother of wounded and tortured souls. It was mystical and magical, and soon I was self-soothing, nurturing my over-firing trauma-filled neurons three times a day.

By age nineteen, when I smoked, my brain started to slip into a horrific, quiet THC-induced paranoid psychosis. Past childhood fears, which my brain had successfully suppressed, were now uber-strong, steroid-like monsters. I hated this new hyper-alert suspicion, so I quit completely—cold turkey.

Alcohol slipped quietly into the vacuum. The magical elixir soothes my over-firing, pain-filled, exploding, terror-like unconscious neurons. I disconnect and swallow—immediate power. I had no idea how awful I felt every day—the darkness I was living—until the contrast: the warmth of the rush, filling inside, engulfing, and cuddling soft-baby me. Cherub-pink, blush angels sang loudly in love, peace, serenity, and calm.

I became a blackout drinker, binge drinking every weekend. I had been arrested twice and crashed and totalled my car on a dark, quiet road at 4 a.m. after passing out. I woke up in tall trees; the windshield smashed in. My door would not open, so I crawled through shattered glass. The accident awakened me to the need to complete my post-secondary education.

Nursing was great, allowing me to distract, avoid, and deny my inner angst. I loved and feared this position; lives were at stake. My brain blowing up, and needing to stuff down images of trauma constantly, is accustomed to overreacting. Pain was now being moulded in a different direction. I was happy to abide, be educated, and follow the thinking of others.

However, I knew what I did not know, but others thought that I did: how to react and provide immediate emergency care for every life-threatening possible blood-curdling situation out there. Exploding childhood neurons of fear, deeply and rigidly ingrained by substance-induced trauma kept me functioning. The chemical release was always on standby, itching for release, chomping at the bit, wanting to be let go, heightened by the impending sense that I was responsible. The awareness that I do not have the knowledge for what I am certain will come out of nowhere, unexpected: bloodletting events, emergency air bubbles, clots, strokes, heart attacks—all events sneaking up on me, exposing me—that I am vulnerable, lost. I don't know what to do. STUPID. FRAUD. INVISIBLE. WANTING. NEEDING SOMETHING. I KNOW NOTHING. RECOGNITION. SEE ME, PLEASE. CONNECT. PROVIDE. PICK ME UP. CRYING BABY. HOLD ME. PLEASE, PLEASE, PLEASE COMFORT ME. PLEASE, I AM HERE. MY ARMS OUTSTRETCHED. WANTING NOTICE. NOT INVISIBLE. ME. SEEN. BUT ALWAYS LYING. HIDING. *SEE ME...* HUG. PLEASE, SOMEONE HOLD AND COMFORT ME...

Scared. I entered another reality. Disconnection is key.

Fentanyl. My long and convoluted STORY; I so much want to please, show, and do not tell. I wrote the words, wanting to expose me.

So much trauma and pain that I had no way of knowing what was happening... my brain right now jumps around, as it should, when in a state of confusion and trying to reach clarity. Trauma is not linear; I am unable to express what happened, why I am, or who I am. My brain, through years of chemical explosions caused by life events, is disordered.

So off it goes, exactly like this—we in recovery call it the squirrel cage—running around, darting about going everywhere, but still annoyingly confined in a seemingly never-ending, going exactly nowhere, always over and over, circular loop.

Fentanyl. I discovered the incredible, eye-opening wonder drug and gasped for more. I overdosed before fentanyl even entered social consciousness. I hid my constant relapsing disorder.

Years before I studied for my graduate nursing degree, I knew that education was key. I mistakenly believed that more knowledge would cure and help me understand why I started to use and why I could not stop. After all, in doing my master's, my focus was on family systems and adolescent substance abuse.

I downed handfuls of white, chalky, easy-to-obtain opiate pills. I knew which over-the-counter pain meds had eight milligrams of codeine. My legal drug of choice, as it converts to morphine in the body. Ten of those tablets, three times a day, kept me high. Then, eight innocuous anti-nausea pills, also easily accessible, at night to sleep. I needed these substances to perform, shove down, deny, smooth out, and mask insecurities inside.

In the morning, swearing never again, I continued the cycle of buying, throwing them down the toilet, and buying again as I continued to use uncontrollably. My addiction neurons grew deeper and stronger, always leading the way to relapsing and using again. Even when I stopped, the neurons remained ingrained, deeply entrenched, still yearning, yawning, and wanting to be filled.

Fentanyl. I overdosed alone.

I discovered discarded narcotic skin patches and applied them all over before bed. I woke up in such a euphoric state and thought, *if I use more patches, I'll hear more wonderful spiritual angels, all singing of peace and awakening.* But then, in the morning, I felt it slowly seeping into my skin, knowing it was moving into my blood. My reptilian and educated brain clicked in. This was the slow march towards the inviting seduction of deep, never-ending, much-needed, but life-ending sleep. I rushed home and tried desperately to scrub those patches off. I made my skin red-raw. I slide down into the tub of hot water, preferring death to exposing my addiction to the world.

I was alone; the bath water swirled around me as I felt myself drift into sleep. I knew if I called 911, it could save me from death. Yet, if others knew what I really was, they would most certainly discover I was nothing but damaged goods, unlovable, dirty, and unclean. Being a drug addict, aka "junkie," as I often read on social media, is not great, so I must hide my horrible identity from others. I fight sleep and the seduction of giving in. I don't die.

I had attended rehab three times in total. I know others have done more, but that was enough for me. I needed more but could never find a solution to stop me from relapsing. I continued to hide who I was from everyone, including myself.

I kept returning to 12-step meetings, eventually finding the power inside me—that is, in every man, woman, and child—a power greater than me. I took charge of myself, took responsibility, spoke my truth, and found my way out. I can share my vulnerability now and expose who I really am.

I apologize to all those I blamed for the decisions I made; to my coworkers, peers, and others. I made amends for my decision to hide. I had no understanding of how deeply caring and compassionate these people were until I finally fully disclosed my alcohol-addicted identity publicly. *(I was a nurse specializing in mental health and addictions of all things.)*

The stigma and shame I felt were only my own. I could not accept who I was until I finally uncovered and exposed all of me. Only now do I know that true freedom comes from no longer hiding in the dark shadows of shame. True freedom comes from standing tall in recovery. Addiction and alcoholism wanted me to keep secrets and isolate. It demanded I not share anything and keep everything bottled up and hidden inside because, after all, this is what drugs do.

I am totally free now, as I take full responsibility and accountability for myself. I uncover, discover, and recover who I am meant to be—I am not my thoughts, as these lie constantly.

I have substance use disorder, which means substances have damaged or disordered my brain. Put a few smatterings of past personal sufferings in there because, after all, trauma also changes the brain.

To recover myself, I must uncover my past, discover what I did, and take responsibility for my conduct and way of being. I have to clean up the wreckage of my past, and when I do so, funny enough, I start to feel "clean."

Yes, some damage was done by others to this brain, but since I want something different, I must take daily action to retrain, reformat, and remodulate this brain. The decades of programming take time to undo. I input new data consistently by listening to the healing words of others.

When people share stories, their words enter my ears and beat drums inside my head—electricity sparks, chemicals react. My neuronal pathways, once drilled down only for addiction, trauma, and pain, are revising. Different connections are made because the brain can change, as it is neuroplastic. I always think of the classic experiment with Pavlov's dog when thinking of my trauma-informed, substance-disordered brain. In this research, food is given whenever a bell rings. This is repeated again and again, and soon, the dog's brain learns that bell-ringing means food. As a result, the dog's body unconsciously responds by salivating whenever it hears a bell ring.

After some time has passed, the food is taken away. The bell continues to ring, and the dog's brain is now conditioned to respond in the same way. Despite the absence of food, salivation still occurs.

This, for me, is why abstinence alone never worked. My brain is habituated, like the dog with this bell. Take away my reward of alcohol or drugs; the neuronal pathways of addiction are still present and remain. Thus, I utilize daily, concentrated action to take conscious control of my brain.

Meditation is key, something I never did despite attending twelve-step meetings. Now, I usually meditate three times per week. I had sponsors, did service work, and had a home group, and yet I still relapsed because I never meditated. Today, I disrupt my parasympathetic nervous system using meditative breathwork: inhale through the nose for a count of five, hold the breath for a count of five, and exhale through the mouth over a count of five. I repeat this three times every morning. This quiets my neurotransmitters, as this busy world of distraction serves to keep many of us sick.

I lie down, close my eyes, and practice full-body progressive relaxation to experience the notion of complete and absolute release. I cannot just think of letting go; my body needs to feel the full somatic expression of letting go. Daily, I access this abundance of peace and allow it to guide me—I am finally in touch with the intuitive power of the e-energy emotions inside. Angry, hostile chickens remain everywhere out there in life, ready to attack, but I am no longer bothered by them. I am finally free, and with gratitude for the first time, I can quietly stand, humble and tall, beside all versions of me.

I trust myself now, which I never could before when alcohol and drugs coursed inside my system, polluting my brain and controlling me. I remind myself daily of the knowledge of a higher and greater power living inside us all.

From ~~Junkie, Addict, Criminal,~~ and ~~Ex-Con~~ to Captain Hamish

by Hamish Roth

It was 1998, and I was in seventh grade—the hardest year of my life. *Little did I know, things would only get harder.* I was bullied every day at school. Even the teachers mocked me, telling my parents I was unteachable. That was when I began to realize I was different. It all started with the teachers mispronouncing my name, which gave the kids fuel to tease me. They'd call me "Ham-ish," like "ham" with "ish," when my name is properly pronounced with a long "a" sound—"HAAmish." Before long, the teasing escalated into much more than just mispronouncing my name.

At that time, we lived on the lower mainland in British Columbia. My family decided to sell our home and move to Vancouver Island, hoping for a fresh start in a *bully-free* community. I attended a Christian private school, and at first, I really liked it. I made some lifelong connections there. However, that year marked the beginning of a troubling period when I experienced sexual abuse for about nine months. It left me deeply confused. As I grew older and entered puberty, everything started to change. I felt lost, unsure of who I was or what I wanted. I questioned my sexuality—wondering if I was gay or straight—and struggled to make sense of it.

Through all of that, I had been on a prescription methamphetamine-based medication (methylphenidate) because of ADHD—since the age of seven. The side effects of paranoia and fear made me awkward socially. I didn't get out as much as the other kids my age and spent a lot of time with my brother, who was 18 months older than me. I would follow him and his friends around.

Eventually, I started making my own friends. Those friendships were strong but few—with how hyper I was, I had a hard time keeping friends. And even at the new school, I found myself getting picked on. I discovered that smoking made me feel better and calmer, so I began smoking anything I could roll up. I would roll up grass and wheat in paper and smoke it like a cigarette. When I first lit up a menthol cigarette, it tasted like candy. Whenever I had the chance to find, steal, or bum a cigarette, I would. I'd even pick up cigarette butts off the ground. By 14 years of age, I started smoking weed. From the first time I smoked a joint, I loved it.

I went away to my first treatment centre, Team Challenge, in my late teens to get off the methamphetamine-based medication and weed in Kelowna, BC. This was the first time leaving my family and flying. I only lasted about a month of the year-long program before taking off from that treatment centre opportunity.

I made my way back to the island. My oldest brother, in the middle of a divorce proceeding, spent his free time partying and using drugs like ecstasy and cocaine. I decided to join him. I used cocaine eleven days straight. I didn't sleep at all during that time and ended up in the hospital with a panic attack/overdose from uppers. This was the first time I felt the serious impact of the drugs. Released from the hospital, my parents told me and my brother we had to decide what we were going to do with our lives and that we couldn't continue using drugs in our family community. My oldest brother and I moved to Alberta for a geographical change. We did the same thing there that we did on the island. We overindulged in drugs and alcohol. That's where I was busted for the first time, charged for fraud and theft. So, I ran back home to my parents.

Once I got back home to the island, I continued smoking weed and hanging around weed circles. I felt like I really fit in. I liked getting stoned; the stories, the camaraderie, I felt like I was part of it all.

One of those friends of mine cuffed (*lent*) me an ounce of weed. That's where my drug dealing started. An ounce turned into two ounces, which turned into a half pound, to a full pound to five, 10, 20 pounds... you see where this is going. During the growth of my weed-selling business, I really started to feel even more wanted and cared about by anybody looking to buy my product. I felt untouchable. I felt popular for the first time in my life, like a celebrity. People bought me drinks at any bar I frequented.

I remember the first time I tried heroin. I looked at the guy who put it on the corner of the dresser for me. I laughed, "Hey man, that looks like a crumb; I'm sure I can handle more than that." My ego and I handled large amounts of cocaine. He told me not to be so cocky and to try it. I sniffed this tiny crumb and melted into a chair for three hours. That little crumb of heroin immobilized me, yet I felt like a thousand pounds of weight had lifted off my shoulders. Then I puked. After vomiting, it felt like nothing mattered. None of my problems mattered—being fat, looking funny, being single, not being good enough—none of those things mattered. I adored the feeling of opiates; I was in love. I didn't even know what heroin was, the dependency on it, or the dope sickness that would follow. I just liked the feeling of oblivion. A few days later, I tried finding opiates again. I ended up finding some methadone, drank that, and woke up five days later.

In the drug trade, I ended up desensitized, like none of this was a big deal. I went from selling marijuana to being a one-stop shop for cocaine, heroin, ecstasy, and marijuana in only a couple of years. You could get anything off me. Well known in my community, it was time to branch out. Once again, I started small, but it quickly escalated. Feeling like a big man, I drove out to Alberta with a trunk full of drugs, sold it all in a few weeks, and made a few grand. It felt good. I turned around, came home, and reloaded. I went back to Alberta with another trunk full of drugs. That time, I met a girl. It felt like anything was possible. I had more money than I'd ever had. People loved when I showed up. I felt incredible. I had respect from everyone, and that was a high in itself.

I decided it was time to move my whole operation to southern Alberta and dive into a relationship with the girl I met. I went back to BC, loaded up all my stuff, grabbed as much weed, cocaine, and heroin as I could, hooked up my SUV and camper, and headed east. In 2010/11, when I showed up in southern Alberta with China white heroin in a community that only had oxy, it blew up... like exploded. Within six months of me being there, property crime went up 60 percent, and they had to open a methadone clinic. In 2011, I was arrested at an airport in British Columbia with a pound of cocaine. The charges were stayed on a technicality. Three weeks later, I was arrested in southern Alberta's biggest heroin bust at the time, which was 10 ounces of China white heroin with a street value of $100,000 dollars. I remember the feeling when those handcuffs went on my wrists—desperation and helplessness. A feeling I learned to become comfortable with in the years that followed. To cover up my fear, I learned to put on one mask after another to fit in wherever I was in the moment. With drug dealers, I acted like a drug dealer. With street people, I acted like a street person. When with church people, I acted like church people. But inside, I felt like I didn't fit anywhere.

Over the next couple of years while waiting for court, I was doing cocaine every day and dabbled with opiates occasionally. I sought a reduced sentence for mental health problems. The crown was asking for ten years. I ended up getting a four-and-a-half-year sentence. In the courtroom that day, I was a lonely, lost, 24-year-old boy going to a "big boy" penitentiary in Drumheller. I was scared. In the prison, I saw people knifed and bleed out. The only thing I had in common with the guys in jail was that we were all fuck-ups in one way, shape, or form.

About six months into serving my sentence, the BC courts brought the stayed cocaine charges back and I pleaded guilty. The judge added two years to my sentence to be served concurrently. Still, four and a half years of incarceration is a long time—long enough to recognize the relationships I had in the drug culture were superficial. None of them actually cared about me. No one came to see me.

When my parole finally rolled around, I had to conform to a bunch of rules. The main rule: *do not use*. As simple as that sounds, I couldn't do it. Over the next year, I was in and out of remand centres, court-appointed treatment centres, and temporary containment centres. I returned to jail four times after being released the first time. I remember that feeling of hopelessness again while I was on parole. I had no friends, my girlfriend cheated on me, I felt like I had no purpose, I didn't belong anywhere—it felt like nobody wanted me. Everybody had moved on with their lives. Nobody waited for me. Even my dog. I felt crushed and heartbroken when she barked at me like she didn't know me. The only people that cared were my family, halfway-house workers, and parole officers.

Lonely, I moved back to BC, served out my parole, and waited for the warrant to expire on my sentence. I lived in an apartment in Victoria then and was about seven months clean, only because it was a requirement of my parole. In 2015, just three days before my birthday, I became a free man without restrictions and conditions. Then my grandfather died on my birthday. I used my grief as an excuse for me to dabble again—I escalated my use in no time. I decided another geographical recovery was in order and loaded up everything I owned in a van and trailer. I moved across the province to Alberta again. Within three months of being back in Lethbridge, I was selling and using cocaine daily, working at the clubs and bars, and being part of the nightlife hanging out with gang members. House parties every night after the bars closed down was a pretty shitty existence that lasted about a year before the police started watching me again. I grabbed my habit and took off back to BC, doing a lot of uppers and playing around with opiates off and on.

When I look back at my life, this was one of the turning points where my addiction was definitely on a wicked roller coaster of highs and lows so bad I wanted to slit my throat. Over the next seven months, I was brutally fucked up, and my family couldn't take it anymore. They begged me to go to treatment. So we filled out applications for treatment centres. When I was accepted to a treatment centre on the lower mainland with a wait list, I booked a recovery house bed while I waited. I bounced around from recovery house to treatment centre, from treatment centre to recovery house. I became well known in the lower mainland and in the recovery community as a "retread" and a "chronic relapser."

Although my sobriety might last only a week to three months, each place gave me little tastes of recovery. The centres I had attended before didn't have that effect because my parents made me go… this time, I was going of my own free will. I was really liking what I was learning about myself and addiction. It was making sense, but then another relapse came, and I was kicked out. Back I went to a recovery house. After leaving one of the houses, I ended up sleeping outside during a storm. I caught pneumonia bad enough to be hospitalized. One of my lungs collapsed, and I was put on life support. I remember the day I was lying in the hospital bed; my best friend beside me was scratching a lottery ticket. (That friend died of an overdose, just four weeks before I wrote this story.) The doctor, dishevelled, panic-stricken, came in with a piece of paper, a release form, which declared, "If you die, the hospital will not be responsible." Apparently, I wasn't getting enough oxygen to my brain. He warned, "If you aren't intubated in the next 10 minutes, you won't wake up."

I turned to my best friend, "What should I do?"

Fear in his eyes, he commanded, "Sign it." The last thing I remember was holding my best friend's hand. I closed my eyes for what felt like an hour. When I woke up, my mom was standing there, makeup smeared, running down her face. She lived five hours away. I had been intubated for over a week. Both my mom and brother had camped out with me for most of those seven days. It took two more months in the hospital for me to heal slowly. Hospital staff helped me transition straight into another treatment centre. I lasted a couple of months before another relapse.

Up and down, in and out, high and straight for another 16 months. Back to my family's house, where once again, I fell into daily use. When my grandmother passed away, my parents came to me and said, "You can't be here doing this, blacking out, and treating our clients like shit."

At my grandmother's funeral in the lower mainland, they planned to leave me there—*and set me free*. I honestly didn't believe they had it in them to do that. I only said, "Yes," because I wanted to call their bluff. I now see things had to get worse before they got better.

The day after the funeral, as Mom drove me to St. Paul's hospital, she reiterated a reminder. "After this appointment, I am going to leave." I was still thinking she didn't really mean what she was saying.

I sat disbelieving anything the doctor could do would help me. However, he gave me a prescription for methadone, asking if I wanted to stop. I told him honestly, I wasn't ready. "When you're ready, come back. I'll help."

I thanked him.

On our way out, mom asked me where I wanted to go. "Let's go see my brother," who was homeless on the downtown east side. When we got there, mom gave me a hug, said she loved me, and then wished me luck. I went along, hugged her back, and told her I loved her, then watched her drive away. I sat on that corner for half an hour, waiting for her to come back. She never did. Hoping for the best, she never expected her two sons would be lost there for the next two years.

In those two years, I didn't leave the six-block radius of Main Street and Hastings down to Abbott Street. My brother and I lived in a single-room occupancy (SRO), rat-infested, 100-year-old building. I sold drugs and hustled merch to survive. My brother and I did everything together: ate together, used together, and even slept in the same bed. Lots of crazy, unbelievable things happened when we were down there. Like the day I returned to the room, and my brother never came home. He was arrested and thrown in jail for the next year. All alone again, I spent the next six months wandering around the lower mainland. Monthly, I suffered infections all over my body, and I was hospitalized a few times a year for my lungs. I hated being alone. I was so tired that I called my parents and asked to come home, making whatever promises I could think of, until they agreed.

One of my promises was to go to therapy. The therapist really helped, and it was better than trying to stay sober on my own. I was on lockdown with my parents, not allowed to go anywhere by myself. Only going out when chaperoned by my parents. And yet, every three to four weeks, I would somehow find a way to use drugs. The counsellor I was seeing at the mental health and addiction centre was able to get me on a waitlist for Cedars, a good treatment centre. This gave me a tiny glimmer of hope. In my mind, I had already been to every government-funded centre on the lower mainland; I was desperate. I heard great things about Cedars—an expensive recovery centre with a few government beds. I was on a six-month waiting list and was doing everything in my power to stay alive while waiting for my opportunity to go.

Once again, I had a few bad relapses, which put me in the hospital. I overdosed more frequently; either the drugs were getting stronger, or I was getting weaker. In March of 2021, I woke up in the Comox Valley hospital after yet another overdose. Once again, my parents told me, "We can't watch you die. You have to figure out what you're going to do while you're waiting to be admitted to the treatment centre."

I called my buddy. "I need a safe place to be, away from anybody who uses." I lived with him and his family on a tiny, secluded island outside of the Nanaimo harbour while waiting for my bed at the recovery centre. Over the next few months, I did okay, and then in the space of one week, I ended up overdosing three times. That week, I called the treatment centre and told them I didn't think I was going to make it to their deadline, and thankfully, they told me they had a bed for me. I remember feeling excited for the first time in a long time. I had the opportunity not to be in pain anymore.

This was my 18th treatment centre, and in my head, my last chance. I told myself that I would submit 100 percent to every rule they had while walking through those doors, and I did. I began to understand myself; I was building a relationship with "Hamish," which was a really cool experience. I learned about my addiction, the way I think, and the way I feel. It was a safe place to really use the opportunity to look at my behaviours. And to learn and heal. I would like to say that's where my recovery came from. But it's not. Two months into the program, I fell and shattered my lower tibia and fibula, requiring surgery.

Waking up after surgery, I called the treatment centre, "I'm ready to come back."

Instead of what I expected, I heard, "You're not coming back. You're on heavy meds, and the centre isn't wheelchair accessible."

Within a week, I was back at my parents' house with a cast on my leg. I clung to my recovery, going to AA meetings in my wheelchair. But it didn't take long before I relapsed. *Déja vu* at my parents' house having a family meeting where they were telling me, "Figure out a plan. You can't stay here after relapsing."

I had a broken leg; it was winter and snowy outside. I called a second-stage recovery house and told them I was just in treatment and broke my leg and needed a second-stage bed. I didn't tell them about my relapse because I was afraid they weren't going to let me in. Once I got there, I had to submit to a dirty urine test. I came clean, told them the truth, and fought to stay. They finally agreed to work with me, but I was on the thinnest ice. That day, I told myself I would do whatever it took to save my life. I made my own personal rules. I wouldn't allow myself to leave the recovery house without a chaperone.

At an AA meeting, I asked a guy to be my sponsor. He gave it to me straight. "Giving back is part of my program. I won't be your friend, but I will take you through the twelve steps." That man took me through the program and saved my life. We spent every day together for the next year doing recovery work and life skills. He taught me how to have genuine relationships. I learned how to love deeply, how to forgive, and how to be forgiven. Most importantly, I learned to forgive myself for all the hell I put myself through. To this day, not only is that man my sponsor, but he's one of my best friends. I stayed at the second-stage recovery house for four months, then I lived with my sponsor for eleven months. During this time, I gave back to the community by working at homeless shelters. I did outreach through the church; I attended multiple meetings and practiced the principles in all my daily affairs. I was truly grasping what having a life with sobriety, meaning, and purpose was like. For work, I did construction on Protection Island, that little Gulf Island where I went to recover. I went back to school and earned the certificates needed for a dream career—to become a ferry captain of a small vessel. At this point, I was over 15 months sober when I finally moved out to Protection Island in the Nanaimo harbour, where I now live.

Around two years into my recovery, I met an amazing woman. We live and work together, supporting each other through our ups and downs. Gaining my sobriety wasn't easy, but it's the best thing I ever did. I still have some difficult days, but I remember and know now that I don't have to use because of them. Some of the most important things I learned from my recovery are some of the most cliché things you'll see on treatment centre room walls. "Easy does it." "One day at a time." "Put the stick down." "Be honest in all your affairs."

Today, because of the hard work I put in and the support that I had from my family, the treatment centres, my community, and my girlfriend, I love myself. At the beginning of my journey, I thought all I could hope for was to stop using drugs. Today, I have a beautiful life.

Recovery gave me more than a life worth living. It gave me a life, period, whereas before I had none. I had kept doing the same things repeatedly, expecting different results. I felt unfixable. I had told myself I tried everything: the easy way, the softer way, the hard way, geographical changes, switching to lighter drugs, using medications, and going to harm reduction. To summarize, I did everything the hard way until I completely submitted and surrendered. At the end, the only thing that worked was complete abstinence and honesty. Such as admitting that my "best thinking/intentions" (promises in the morning not to use) almost always ended up with me high. It used to be that all roads led to drugs. Now no roads lead to drugs. The most vital step for me was finding a responsible member of the program to guide me through the steps.

Today, I am nearing my three-year cake. Looking at my life, I am full of gratitude. I went from Hastings Street to an ocean-front property with my Harley, a beautiful fiancé, and a life I never imagined possible.

I am dedicating this story to Jason David Love, born February 25, 1985, who overdosed and died March of 2024. He was my absolute best friend, and I am grieving his passing healthfully, without using any drugs. I honour him by staying sober.

I want to thank everybody for reading my story, and if you're struggling, reach out. Never give up on yourself. You are worth it. If I can do it, you can do it too. It's okay to ask for help.

Sincerely, Senior Captain Hamish Roth

Out of the five people in my core friend group, only three of us are still alive, and I've lost over 30 other friends to drug addiction.

*L*OST GIRL

by Stacy Zeman

When you tell someone that you come from a dysfunctional home, the stereotypical mental picture is one of drug-addicted parents, a living environment littered with broken furniture and kids in dirty clothes, crying, left to fend for themselves... and while that is definitely one scenario, there is another type of dysfunctional family that is much less obvious. They live in neighbourhoods everywhere—even wealthy, high-class, gated communities—and on the outside, they look normal and happy.

My family was one of those—*normal*. A mom and a dad, two kids, and sometimes a dog. We lived in a nice home on the same street as all of the other *normal* families. Doing all of the *normal* things that the other families did: going to school and work, spending weekends with friends, camping, playing sports, and other such *normal* and even somewhat privileged things.

But there was one thing that was a little less *normal* about us... and that was how the people in my family expressed their love to one another.

Growing up, I never really saw my mom and dad act like two people who cared about each other. In fact, it was quite the opposite. There was a lot of blaming, shaming, and name-calling that made life often feel quite miserable. I never understood, based on my childish idea of what a family was supposed to be, why they treated each other like this, why they would never hug or kiss each other. There always seemed to be an underlying air of tension that I couldn't quite put my finger on, but it was something that I always felt.

I got the impression from a very early age that my brother wasn't my biggest fan either, which made the tension described above even more challenging for me to hold in my system.

If I had to describe how it felt to be both a daughter and a sister in the family environment that I was raised in, I would say that it was a roller coaster ride of reactivity and aggression at times and icy coldness and avoidance at others. Either way, it almost always felt cutting.

As a child who felt deeply and having nothing else to compare it to, I assumed that what I was experiencing as love was *normal*, and still, on a subconscious level, I always knew that it was supposed to feel different. The love that I received almost always hurt, and love was something that was supposed to make you feel good. Accepted. Understood.

Love was supposed to make you feel like you belonged somewhere, not like you needed a barf bag.

I didn't know it then, but love in its true form was something that my family didn't know how to give or receive. This took me decades in therapy to realize and is now something that I understand isn't actually all that uncommon. Unfortunately, as a little girl, there was no way for me to know that, never mind understand... so my only conclusion as a child was to adopt the belief that I was unlovable, useless, worthless, and deeply flawed.

Growing up the way I did, having nothing else to compare my life to and knowing no different, I was led to believe that my family was normal—and that all of my problems were problems because I was the problem. I was unlovable, not because my family wasn't able to express love in a healthy way, but because there was something wrong with me. That I was the problem seemed like the only explanation that made sense. I lived with that understanding for decades.

Looking back now, I can clearly see that I never had a chance of a normal life. And so I would like to say this: healing from something that you never recognized as trauma in the first place is like being asked to solve a puzzle without any of the pieces.

With substance abuse, it's usually too late when people realize that there's even an issue. But I would argue—because I love a good debate—that if the environment is attuned, there would be someone who would recognize the signs along the way.

Gabor Maté says that the opposite of addiction isn't sobriety, that it's connection. He says that all addictions are attempts to soothe some kind of pain, and that dealing with addiction requires addressing this pain, which he claims can be done by being supported by and connecting to others. So people aren't addicted to drugs or alcohol, sex, shopping, food, or exercise… They are addicted to escaping reality.

As someone who has personally struggled with substance abuse issues for one half of my entire life, while I wholeheartedly agree with Gabor Maté, I would also say that there's a deeper layer that sits below the surface of connection, and that is a person's self-worth. For me, not feeling safe in my life and unable to connect with others in a healthy way made me feel like a terrible, worthless person.

My entire life, as far back as I can remember, I felt like I was somehow broken or flawed. The majority of my life, I didn't even feel like I belonged as a girl. I didn't feel like a boy either, even though I was more comfortable with the idea of being one. Sometimes I didn't even feel like a human being.

In third grade, I can remember hiding myself in the change room, afraid of the other girls finding out that I wasn't like them. If they saw me, they would know for sure that there was something wrong with me. On the outside, I may have looked the same; I liked to play in similar ways, and of course, I had the same anatomy. But deep down at my core, I felt like I somehow just didn't belong. That there was nothing that I could do, that I would never fit in because I was somehow missing what it took. In hindsight, what I lacked was a core belief that I had any value as a human being. I had zero self-worth, but underneath it all, even deeper, is that I was missing me.

As early as fourth grade, I remember making plans to take my dad's hunting rifles out of the locked gun closet so I could kill all the members of my family in their sleep and then kill myself. I wanted to die because living was too painful, but I worried that taking my own life would hurt my family too much; by killing all of us, I wouldn't have to worry about it. The only kink in the plan was that I didn't know how a gun worked. In hindsight, now that I've experienced what the other side of life has to offer—the side that is more than just a suffocating black hole—thankfully, I never committed such atrocities.

Fast-forward to my high school debut, and like many other kids, that's when things really went off the rails for me. In eighth grade, I was a high-achieving student and a talented athlete. I never really had to study or try in school; it was all effortless. I was super-talented and lived and breathed to play sports, basketball in particular. During my first year of high school, I was asked to play up on the ninth-grade team, and even then, I still dominated. Looking back, it's safe to say that I loved playing sports because, when I was immersed in the game, I didn't have time to think about all of the things that were wrong with me. As a bonus, I received positive attention and validation for my athleticism. It made me think that maybe I was not so bad of a person after all.

If things had gone another way, I definitely would have had a future as some kind of athlete. I was smart and talented, and though I didn't realize it at the time, I was also pretty. But none of that mattered. In fact, it only made things worse. When I would express how much I hated myself, instead of receiving validation that I was experiencing some kind of pain, people would bypass my feelings with an adhesive bandage—telling me I was smart, pretty, and talented, as if there was no reason for me to feel anything other than lucky to be alive.

My pain was never validated, and my voice was never heard, even when I screamed, so I repressed my anger further, causing me to question reality and reaffirm that the problem was something within me.

It didn't take long for me to find the other kids who were in pain. They were hanging out at the smoke pit dressed like skateboarders and goths. Slumped over with their sunken eyes, trying to look invisible and skipping classes to get drunk and high... doing the bare minimum just to make it through another day.

By the time ninth grade ended, I was smoking pot all day, every day, most of the time getting high before first class even started and then doing whatever I needed to do in order to keep that going throughout the rest of the day. We travelled in a pack and hid in alleyways and behind convenience stores to smoke.

On weekends, we would get someone's older sibling or a homeless person to buy us alcohol and other drugs like acid, mushrooms, ecstasy, and cocaine. We had no awareness of the side effects of those drugs, never mind giving thought to the purity. We could always hang out at the home of one friend or another whose parents didn't really care that much or seemed to notice that we were all fucked up.

We got into all kinds of trouble. We used to ditch cabs to get around. We would tell the cab drivers that our money was inside the house at some random address near where we wanted to go. When we got out of the cab, we ran through the yard, then on to wherever it was that we were really going—leaving the cab driver just sitting there, unpaid for his work. We would steal things, destroy property, and start fights. One of the kids I was hanging out with even shot someone at a house party. Somehow, the madness of living this way carried on all through high school.

The people that I was hanging out with weren't really my friends; they were just people to get drunk and high with. The reason we all liked each other wasn't because we were connected on a deeper level, or any level for that matter. We liked each other because there was always someone who had the resources to help us all numb our pain.

For me, these addictions and self-destructive behaviours were never really about the pleasurable side-effects. It was more a desperate attempt for me to stop feeling the pain of being so flawed. It was my attempt to stop feeling the pain of being such a terrible, worthless person.

There were a couple of times when my mental health got awful and I ended up on the psych ward. I would stay for a few days in my own little padded room with all of the other mentally unwell people until the storm would blow over. (By storm, I mean my wanting to kill myself.) When I'd get out, I'd tell my friends that I had missed school because I had just been really sick, then resume business as usual. Getting into as much trouble as we possibly could, wherever we could. Smoking. Drinking. Doing drugs. Leaving a trail of destruction wherever we went.

I was one of the few who managed to scrape by somehow and make it through grade twelve. From my class of almost 700 kids, there were only four of us in my group of friends who made it all the way to graduation.

The same day that I graduated from high school, I left home. I couldn't wait to get out of there. I was 18 years old at the time, and because that was the legal drinking age in Alberta, I thought that Calgary would be an ideal place to start my new life. In less than eight weeks in Alberta, I found myself thrown in jail twice and hospitalized three times. The final straw for my Albertan residency came when I stole my own car from the designated driver who had offered to take care of me one night. We had stopped to get gas, and while she was inside paying, I jumped into the driver's seat and took off. Driving my car blackout-drunk down the wrong side of the highway, I drove full speed into oncoming traffic, causing a major collision and impacting the lives of several innocent people—forever.

The next day, I woke up oblivious to what had happened. The hospital had released me in the early hours of the morning, so I woke up in my bed at home with two black eyes and what appeared to be a broken nose. Thinking it must have been a wild night, I grabbed my keys and headed outside to go to work, only to find that my car wasn't there.

This wasn't the first time that I had lost my car or forgotten where I'd parked it after a wild night, so I wasn't worried. Yet there was this familiar sense of dread that I wasn't going to be able to piece together the fragmented memories that I needed to find it.

After doing some extremely painful detective work, feeling as hungover and removed from reality as ever, I found out that my car was at a local tow yard. Still unsure of what had happened the night before, there was one thing that I was sure of: I was going to get my car so that I could get to work. I called a cab.

When I got to the tow yard, I thanked the taxi driver for the ride and went inside to pay the impound fee to the attendant on shift. He directed me to the lot full of cars, and it was my understanding that I was to walk the lot until I found my vehicle and then see myself out.

It took me a few laps of the place before I finally found my car. Probably because I was still a little drunk and freshly concussed, but also because my car looked more like something you'd see at a scrap yard than a car lot.

The realization that I had totalled my car was extremely sobering, and it was in that moment that I recognised the reality of my situation. I had to leave town.

Without a car and now a warrant out for my arrest, which is a complicated story in and of itself, I had to consider where I could live... somewhere that I wouldn't need a car or a drivers licence to get by. I was really into snowboarding at the time and decided that Whistler would be the place.

Boy was it something—by something, I mean a blur of barely getting by, drunken nights, broken bones, more head injuries, and more mistakes— that fortunately were less costly than some of those that came before in terms of my criminal record but were just as costly in terms of the toll on both my physical and mental health.

I survived on gas station spring rolls, instant breakfast packets, cigarettes, cheap beer, and bong hits that were a mix of weed and tobacco. My two best friends were strippers. I spiralled deeper into a self-made abyss. When the end of the month came and I was short on rent, I'd phone my mom for money to cover the difference. When she supplied the funds, it checked the box: my parents still love me.

I never once thought of the special kind of hell it must have been for them to receive phone calls from police stations and hospitals in the middle of the night, which were pretty much the only other updates they received about me.

There wasn't one big moment that changed everything for me, though for the sake of this story, I wish that there was. I never really hit a big rock-bottom because I'd been residing there my entire life. After long enough, I guess I just got sick of hating myself. Of waking up feeling like shit. Of walking around feeling worthless and out of my skin. Constantly stressed out, just trying to merely survive another day. What was the point if this was all there was? There had to be more.

By the grace of God, I connected with a psychologist who had an office in West Vancouver, and I started going down to the city to see him once a month. I have a vague recollection of my first session with him. I was dressed in all black, with eyes to match. I sat the entire 60 minutes on the chair in his office, curled into myself, never looking up from the safety of myself the entire time. But I didn't hate him. And I didn't hate what he had to say either; in fact, I hung on to every word he said.

He was the first person in my life to validate my pain. He told me he understood and that everything made sense. He told me that he was sorry and that I didn't have to feel like this, that there were things we could do to make me feel better—to not wake up every day hoping that I'd die.

Eventually I learned to trust him.

One day early in our relationship, he dropped an F-bomb and told me about how he used to snort cocaine. This confession totally won me over. He wasn't just some nerdy shrink. He'd been through it too. If he got through it, surely so could I.

He told me that I had to start eating healthier because your gut feeds your brain. While a better diet might not fix all my problems, I certainly wasn't doing myself any favours by hoping to meet all of my nutritional needs by relying on gas station spring rolls and instant breakfast packets.

At one point, I even started to look forward to seeing him. And while I know my mother paid him, he listened to me with open curiosity—he wasn't there to judge or criticize. He took my brain and my heart, laid it all out on the table, and helped me to make sense of everything. But beyond that, it was the first time that I felt safe and seen in a relationship with another human being. Over the course of a decade, I went from being that little black-eyed, curled-up ball in his chair to what I would call a fully-functioning human.

After years of waking up almost every single day wishing that I would die, I finally liked myself enough that I saw value in living. I continued drinking, which was still a serious problem for me, but for the first time since "entering into the tunnel" early on in high school, I actually wanted to be alive.

Eventually I moved back to my hometown, Kelowna, to give my liver a break from drinking every day and night and to see what it would be like to "get a real life." Living in Whistler as a young adult is kind of what it would be like to live inside an amusement park as a kid. It felt very much like I was living in the land of make-believe. Kelowna meant spending time in reality, which I felt had the potential to set me on a different path.

It was at that point that I stopped seeing that first therapist, as it was just too far to travel. But that one safe relationship and the validation I received from him had built enough of a foundation for me to continue doing my own work. Having finally completed my master's degree in suffering, I was moving on.

I became just as committed to my healing as I had been to the drugs and alcohol. I read every book about addiction, mental health issues, and the mind-body connection that I could get my hands on. I did acupuncture and delved into energy medicine and shadow work. In my spare time, I attended workshops and trainings, learning everything there was to learn about myself and how I'd ended up where I'd ended up.

I went all in on myself—nothing could detour me. At this point, I was really into exercise and yoga. Although I have to admit yoga was initially a way to cope, another crutch, but it was also a gateway. A healthy one that propelled me forward. I became obsessed with learning about the power of the subconscious mind, attachment theory, the human nervous system, manifestation, and how it all relates to life as we know it. My research gave me the power to change.

Eventually, I opened a fitness studio and later a yoga studio. Both continued to lead me step-by-step back to the truth of who I am and always have been. As I continued to gain more access to the parts of myself that I had rejected, exiled off, hidden, and forgotten about during childhood, I started to get to know myself, and I started to understand everything. Finally, I had some of the pieces to the puzzle...

I realized that the programming that I had received early in life was that love hurts. That life hurts. That people and relationships hurt. I would never be good enough, bright enough, or successful enough. Therefore, nothing mattered, and I didn't matter to myself. The people that I wanted so badly to see me, to love me, to accept me simply weren't capable, and so it makes total sense that I abandoned almost every part of who I was in a desperate attempt to merely be tolerated. But the cost of this was that I sacrificed my entire self. I was only a shell of a human.

I realized that I had never felt secure, or like I could trust people, in any relationship, and given what I had experienced as relational dynamics growing up, it was impossible for me to feel secure within myself or to trust myself, so it's no wonder that I wanted to die!!! I had basically been untethered, drowning, and wearing a mask my entire life.

In a come-to-Jesus moment, because nothing really stood out in the days or weeks leading up to this, I woke up on the morning of September 17, 2017, and I stopped drinking. It was strange and bizarre and completely unexpected. The only explanation that I have is that I had finally done enough healing, reparenting, and reprogramming of my subconscious mind that my frequency was no longer a vibrational match with the lower energies of alcohol. And just like that, alcohol and the need for it, the craving, the drive, the grip it had held in my life for almost two decades, all disappeared.

I've now been sober for almost seven years, and if you asked me how I got to this place, I would have to tell you that I learned to love myself and that once I started to love myself, alcohol just stopped agreeing with me. I didn't even try to quit. I literally woke up that day, a day just like every other day, and my need to drink was gone. Not only was it gone, but I actually couldn't drink if I tried—because believe me, I've tried!!! I immediately feel sick and out of my body. Which is a feeling that I no longer enjoy.

The alcohol went, and in the years to follow so did all of the sacrificing of my "self," the trying to fit in, to be someone that could be loved and accepted. After years of shrinking to fit into a box that would never be my size, the constant pain of rejecting myself finally became greater than the pain of facing the rejection that I had always felt—but was never strong enough to face—from my family.

I finally realized that I wasn't deeply flawed, but rather that the people who surrounded me while growing up weren't capable of loving themselves, never mind capable of loving me the way that I needed to be loved.

I know that most people's sobriety stories involve some kind of pivotal moment, but I genuinely believe that before that day, the drugs and alcohol had offered nothing other than pain relief for me. Once I got to a place in my life where that pain no longer needed to be relieved—not only did my body not need or want it anymore—my body rejected it.

If my theory of addiction being a loss of self is correct, I had finally found what I needed to get sober. I had found myself.

www.mindbodyrizz.com

Living Proof of the Maverick Protocol

by Taylor Pridy

My path through recovery has been a journey of revelation, focusing intensely on the present while peering into the shadows of my past. I've come to realize the profound impact of Adverse Childhood Experiences (ACEs) on shaping one's path towards addiction. Previously, I believed such experiences were confined to extreme cases of abuse or neglect. Yet, as my recovery deepens, I've unearthed truths about myself—both enlightening and disquieting—through heightened self-awareness. This process isn't just about acknowledging personal shortcomings; it's about understanding how the patterns of those around us contribute to how we shape our choices and patterns that we later duplicate in our addiction.

Growing up in the quiet outskirts of a small town, my childhood seemed *normal* at times. Yet, a pivotal encounter at the age of four shattered that façade. At the park with my mother, I glimpsed a man—my biological father—bruised and broken, a victim of his own demons. Later, random encounters consisted of bumping into him at the grocery store every four to six years. It created a perspective tinged with the residue of neglect that left me grasping for understanding and closure. Thankfully, David, my stepfather, was in our lives, a beacon of stability and love, steering me away from potential darkness and towards a life anchored in purpose.

David could have succumbed to an easier, darker path, filled with motorcycles and easy money, but instead, he chose to nurture and protect. His love for motorcycles and the art he created on them sparked an early fascination of mine towards drawing and painting at a young age. It was one of the few positive influences amidst the haze of our secluded existence. He supported and encouraged my art, so much so it made me believe I would become a famous airbrush or tattoo artist. Though my parents didn't drink alcohol, our household hummed with the scent of cannabis, a choice my parents made consciously, yet one that eventually shaped my perception of coping and self-medication.

Childhood curiosity drove me to experiment with substances from a young age. At ten, I reluctantly tried cannabis with my sister, five years my senior. In retrospect, she was trying to scare me off from using any substance. It worked for five years. Then, at 15, I smoked more out of peer pressure than personal desire. By then, my quest for existential understanding led me to delve into psychedelics, influenced by early encounters with what I now recognize as childhood "night terrors." These experiences of navigating multidimensional realities at a young age initially instilled fear but also fuelled a deep curiosity. The allure of altering my perception became a delicate balance between exploration and escapism. Growing up with a mother struggling with mental illness and believing in the potential genetic influence on my own destiny, I felt compelled to unravel the mysteries of the mind. This exploration offered both a quest for understanding and a justification to push the boundaries of human consciousness without feeling reckless.

At nineteen, an ill-fated collision during a reckless descent on my BMX left me with shattered bones and a prescription containing hydrocodone. What followed was a downward spiral into the abyss of addiction. The pills, initially a respite from physical agony, morphed into a lifeline tangled with the insidious grip of heroin. What began as an attempt to manage pain escalated into a battle for control, punctuated by cycles of euphoria, agony, and confusion.

I returned to work after my medical E.I. payments ended. I was still using. I knew something had to change. Other drug users pointed me towards an addiction clinic. There, I experienced buprenorphine for the first time. Touted as a lifeline, hoping for some sort of saviour or relief, it just plunged me deeper into despair with its unforeseen torment called, "precipitated withdrawal." It was horrible—I experienced a chemically induced withdrawal from a medication that blocked opiate receptors, leaving me with no way to get high and having to suffer through the withdrawal. Instead of a saviour, I was hurting as the "medication" fast-tracked me into heightened withdrawal symptoms. Misunderstood and forsaken, I found solace in self-medicating again. The veneer of recovery shattered under the weight of misjudgment and prejudice, leaving me adrift in a sea of self-doubt as I watched my symptoms of withdrawal be misunderstood. They misread my recovery attempts and labelled me as an active user. I lost my job.

Rescue came in the unexpected form of family intervention—a lifeline extended by a sister's unwavering love and a brother-in-law's steadfast support. A summer in Prince George offered respite, a chance to reclaim lost ground. Yet, my understanding of recovery remained confined to mere abstinence rather than true transformation.

With that false perception guiding me, I spent years in refineries and oilfield camps in Prince George and Fort St. John. I was surrounded by a culture of excess, where substance abuse masked the ache of isolation and unfulfilled potential. Yet, I convinced myself that the wild amount of hours I worked directly correlated with how well I was doing with my addiction. I figured if I was working 70-90 hours a week, then I must be doing good. I was wrong; it just blurred the lines between work and debauchery. Work became a fleeting respite from a self-destructive vicious cycle of years of substance use on days off and withdrawal when back to work.

One week after I left camp-work, my grandmother passed away. Two weeks later, my dad passed away. A "contact" said he had a job for me in a "business," which turned out to be a front, to lure me into the underbelly of the drug scene. Within months, I went from making good money pipefitting to making even more money from crime.

That became my life. I wasn't just addicted to the drugs; I was dealing and addicted to the lifestyle that came with it. The money, power, and respect overrode my physical addiction and gave me just enough of an incentive to stay sober for a few months. This joke of a lifestyle convinced my family and others that I was doing well. I rationalized I must have my life together because I was making a large amount of money. The more money I made, the more I wanted. Unknowingly, I was trying to fill an empty hole inside me, not with recovery and self-awareness but meaningless interactions and large amounts of money.

This charade had a disastrous impact on my mental well-being. It was only a matter of time before I was trading the drugs I handled for my drug of choice—opiates of any kind. It progressed from there. In the worst ways you could imagine, which I detail and reveal in my upcoming book, *Destroying the Myths of Addiction with the Magic of Recovery*.

I lost everything repeatedly: the new condo, new cars, new truck, storage units—ALL GONE. My life skipped across rock bottom; I faced homelessness and despair. I was still blind as to what I really needed to escape this life. For some reason, I subconsciously thought I'd quit cold turkey one day and be done. This single thought shaped my entire outlook on addiction and recovery. Years of gang violence, being set up, sucker-punched, attacked with machetes, extortion, defamation of character, and often barely escaping with my life, along with the fear of law enforcement catching up with me, finally gave me the incentive to attempt another change.

Another cure move should do it. I left everything. With just a backpack, I moved to another town, another province. I ended up crashing on Mom's couch in her one-bedroom apartment. For the first time, I looked at recovery programs. When I learned they required complete abstinence, I didn't even consider that route an option. Maybe I could use cannabis to self-medicate the pain and craving of withdrawal to quit opiates. It had worked for my dad, who used this tactic to quit heroin cold-turkey after five years. I had clung to my false belief that weed was all I needed; after all, it is a healing plant. What I ended up doing was going to the local addiction clinic, while still using. I figured devoting myself to a "legitimate" full-time job while taking methadone and using cannabis at night was my way out. Then before I knew it, I was doing the exact same thing I always did, but this time with the support of the "system"—a doctor gave me my drugs every day—methadone. The power it had on me was identical to the street opiates. The high dose kept me numb; recovery programs and N/A were mere suggestions. I found a construction job, and all I did was work 10-hour-days and take methadone.

Life seemed alright; things were stabilizing again. I was making money and had purchased a commuter car. But with those steps forward, my methadone dose progressed to taking 290 ml a day. Clueless, I felt I was progressing—even though I could pat myself on the back for not being on street drugs—I was still hooked. Clearly, I didn't know what recovery was. Once again, I was trying to work my addiction away... I made it about a year, when I was laid off from the construction job. With no actual recovery work done, I had attracted the wrong crowd, which got me kicked out of mom's apartment, largely due to the people I hung out with causing havoc. I ended up homeless, out of work, and back on street drugs. During this time, I was arrested for sleeping in my car three times, and my car was impounded.

I found myself drifting from one shelter to another, each more temporary than the last, until I was blacklisted from them all. My past, a relentless shadow I desperately tried to escape, continued to haunt me, undermining my every effort. No matter how much I struggled to change on my own, without the deeper recovery work, it seemed the world refused to look past my history, harassing me at every turn and denying me the peace I so desperately sought. I was pushed to the streets. I couldn't even camp on the river without my stuff being robbed or my tent being burned down when I left to source out a fix or go to the food bank. It didn't matter how much I tried to mind my business. When you are homeless, you lose your privacy to everyone who wishes to invade your space. Waking up to shovels in the face, pepper spray, and many more horrible things you wouldn't think a person would keep subjecting themselves to—yet, it keeps happening! You might think a life like this would push me to make a drastic change to want out, but that's not how the addictive lifestyle works. The terrible things that happen to you somehow create an even stronger magnetic pole to suck you back in and keep you in the clutches of even deeper, darker addictions. The more horrible my environment became, the more my mental health declined. Yet at the time, the drugs convinced me that it's all part of the program of using and what I must do to get a regular supply and avoid endless dope sickness.

I felt like the whole world was designed to work against me and my chances of success. I didn't know how to reach out, so I didn't. I stopped contact with my sister, niece, nephew, and brother-in-law. The last thing I heard her say ruminated in my head over and over: "I'm accepting your impending death. It's too much for me to keep watching you self-destruct."

Through some level of hazy empathy, I saw the emotional terror I was putting my family through with my bouncing back and forth from sobriety to addiction and danger. As if that didn't have a strong enough impact, I was homeless in the same town as my mother. The gaslighting, gang stalking, extortion, entrapment, and defamation of character were impacting my mother's and family's lives—not just my own. An embarrassment to my family, I was filled with shame.

Acknowledging this while wracked with pain from my mouth full of abscessed teeth added to the realization I needed to make a change or die. Throughout my eleven years of addiction, many people overdosed around me, needing naloxone or CPR. Spared again and again, I concluded that wasn't going to be how I died. I honestly believed I was invincible and couldn't die, and that not only was I stuck in a life of addiction, but my twisted dope-addled brain told me that it was my destiny. When my family shared they were accepting my inevitable death, I realized I was already dead to them. Seeing my life end through their eyes, I had to admit my physical death was imminent. This wake-up call penetrated all my denial. I communicated I wanted to get off the drugs for real this time.

I broke the silence. In a vulnerable moment, sitting in a shopping mall parking lot in my mom's car, I talked to my sister on speaker phone. Her words gave me hope. "You don't know how much everyone misses you. Your niece and nephew want their uncle back. You don't know how often I think about you. How I believe in you."

The two of them gave me hope. Britney planted the idea that once I left addiction behind, I was going to help others. She even suggested, "You're going to write a book about all the crazy things that happened." That idea I might be able to utilize my unfortunate existence to help others heal from addiction ignited a spark. That was a flame I could fan and breathe in. In that moment, where I felt so defeated and consumed with addiction, I began to believe in myself.

Shortly after, I reached out to whatever resources I knew to be available; I got a referral from the addiction clinic to a detox centre. After waiting, calling, waiting, and tapering off heroin, meth, and fentanyl, I finally got into the Phoenix Detox Centre in Kamloops. This was a huge leap for me, especially because I avoided all detox centres during my entire addiction for a reason. Every other time I chose to try withdrawal, I believed all the help I needed was weed. Detox centres didn't allow pot.

At some level, I knew I needed cannabis or I wouldn't make it. Discrete cannabis vape products enabled me to make it through to the end of my detox stay. I let them assume that the THC stored in my fat cells, showing up past the initial urine test, was from before I received a bed there. Staying and managing the withdrawals were super difficult, but what was I going to do when it came time to leave?

The universe had my back, though, when I was offered an assessment with a woman from the Maverick Supportive Recovery Centre. This amazing person provided another dash of hope by treating me like a normal person when nobody else saw me. She told me of their extensive programming that felt intimidating but super intriguing. The centre had just created a new program—the first in the world—a non-impairing cannabis study for harm reduction and opiate agonist therapy in liaison with Thompson Rivers University and the University of British Columbia—a sign from the universe.

First, I had to pass the tests and trials, proving I truly did want recovery bad enough because that centre had a five-month waiting list. I could see the light. I wanted to stay clean while waiting for a spot at the Maverick. I called about availability every few days till my phone was stolen. Though the only thing I had in my tool belt was buprenorphine, I still felt more confident than ever before. I stayed sober and went to NA meetings. But I needed more. I knew the challenges of the homeless environment all too well. I did what it took to get into detox again. After a horrible 11 days, my addiction doctor decided she was going to put me on the injectable slow-release version of buprenorphine that lasts a minimum of 30 days. Reluctant, it was one of the best choices that was made for me. With opiate receptors blocked, there was no way to get high anymore. Taking this medication enhanced my chances of getting into Maverick.

Out of detox a second time, again, no options but back onto the street while I waited to get into the Maverick Support Recovery Centre. No more messing around. This 11-year-old game of constant withdrawals in my body had to end. I was in pain, lost, and confused. I wanted out this time for good. I was ready and knew I had to face the pain. Every bridge burnt but the Maverick, and it sounded like it was made for me. Every suggestion the Phoenix Centre and the assessment team from the Maverick gave, I followed. Still in withdrawal and pain, I had my mother's support. Seeing my effort, she allowed me to sleep in her car and brought me food and edibles. I locked the doors and slept. I felt supported. Things were aligning—proof my path was destined. I couldn't ignore the signs. I met a successful Maverick client at a NA meeting a block from where I slept. The things he shared about the centre inspired me to persevere. Even though I was smoking all day and using edibles to sleep, I still went to the meetings. I overheard someone whisper, "Is he even allowed to be here?" I stunk like weed. It didn't phase me; I knew I HAD to be there; it kept me on the path.

Two weeks later, I was accepted to the Maverick, where I finally learned and dove into what recovery truly meant. It felt strange and unreal. Hungry for real change, I refused to waste this opportunity.

I am grateful for being led to this centre, with its diverse recovery methods as well as a supportive personalized recovery plan. Attending the many different mandatory groups was intimidating at first. Within a week, despite my nervousness, I opened up, engaged, and even enjoyed the groups, moving past my initial resistance. The Maverick not only had the familiar AA and NA, it had groups such as: Life Ring Secular Recovery, Discovery, Recovery Dharma, Health & Wellness, a two-hour Daily Addictions Recovery Program (D.A.R.P.), Wellbriety, Land Based Teachings, an anxiety group, yoga, a physical activity group, a Relating in Recovery group, Therapeutic Art, and a counsellor available for all phases.

My authentic enthusiasm for recovery was about to be derailed by one problem that had the power to steal away my ability to continue. Most of my teeth were cracked, and many were extremely abscessed, swelling up my whole face and wracking me with unimaginable pain. Extraction wasn't an option because the infection was too high. When antibiotics didn't work anymore, the doctors had to prescribe penicillin, saying, "Your allergic reaction can't be worse than the state you're about to hit if we can't stop the infection."

Almost in septic shock, not eating or sleeping, and in extreme agony, I had no reserves of strength left or an ability to focus on the programs. My addict self reared its ugly head, wanting to escape the pain and tempting me to veer off the recovery path. Pain, both physical and emotional, was just too much to bear. It was a battle internally with my sober-self and my addict-self. Mental agony followed the physical agony, wondering which self was going to win. It was hell to aim for sobriety and stability, facing two more months of all-encompassing pain before I could join Phase Two: the cannabis program.

That next phase required zero breaches. The infection stole my clear thinking, my ability not to react, and my communication towards the staff became aggressive. An absolute deal breaker for treatment. I faced rejection again. I felt hopeless, drowning in the physical pain. If this was existence, I wanted out. Yet in these defeating moments, rather than leave and self-medicate the only way I knew how, I chose to stick with recovery. Sitting outside on the bench, wrestling with the devil of addiction amidst the haze of pain and hopelessness—weighing my options to leave, to get high, to throw all my chances away just to escape the pain—was witnessed. Watching through a window, the coordinator recognized in me a determination. This was the biggest synchronicity of all. Just as I chose the path of recovery over addiction, she saw this was the time for an exception.

Under program supervision, being allowed to utilize medical cannabis for pain management during my teeth extraction helped me return to a semblance of stability. Also, the logistics of the licensed prescription and being designated as a licensed patient removed the stigma of "using" and kept me on the recovery path.

My recovery took even greater strides when I met a clinical counsellor, Michael Kohen, a medical professional from the CannSolve Clinic, Kamloops, BC. I had no idea what to expect. He arrived with his signature box of coffee, two boxes of Timbits, and a cooler filled with cannabis products. I thought, *This is the guy that changes the world of recovery for all of us!* We have been waiting for other options that aren't methadone, extended release morphine, hydromorphone, and all the other things you get *prescribed* for sleep, anxiety, depression, ADHD, etc. Most of these drugs fall under the umbrella of Opiate Agonist Therapy; in my experience, they are another form of addiction that traps too many of us seeking true recovery. Two stigmas exist still that must be eradicated to accelerate our work in recovery. The first is that prescriptive harm reduction drugs are not always accepted in abstinence-based recovery programs, and others in recovery that never used the harm reduction method have been known to shame others on the prescriptions. Shaming is unacceptable and harmful beyond belief to someone who needs that first step or their journey to recovery ends before it begins.

The second stigma to remove is even more vital in my mind. Superior in every way to the pharmaceuticals that have dominated the recovery scene for far too long, medicinal cannabinoids deserve to be more widely accepted. Access to acidic forms of cannabis was crucial to my recovery.

The pioneer in this field to bring awareness to the healing potential of cannabis is Michael. My first encounter with him was unlike anything I've encountered before. We sat at a table with his coffee and donuts, just like regular recovery meetings. What he said to all of us was different from any other recovery model. His philosophy was that **people matter**. "We need stability to recover. I focus on three things: pain management, sleep, and quality of life." He knew we could go to five or six groups or meetings a day for recovery, but none of it would stick if we were dealing with pain, tired from lack of rest, or too foggy from the prescribed meds to focus and engage properly in the healing support programs.

Cannabis is an alternative that shows many advantages over the typical prescribed harm reduction drugs. I'd never even heard of the science behind CBDA and THCA oils and how CBDA was not only a non-psychoactive substance, it was so much more. It's also an analgesic (pain relief), anti-inflammatory, antibacterial, and antioxidant.

At the time of my teeth extraction, I was taking CBDA along with the once-a-month injectable slow-release version of buprenorphine shot along with sleeping pills. Two weeks after I had my dental work done, the dentist said I was healing twice as fast as most people. I was still a full-pack-a-day cigarette smoker. Within six months, I was able to taper off the sleep meds by using Michael's THCA pills and oils, aided significantly by the recovery tools I learned in the groups. It only took two months to be free of the sleep meds completely, thanks to the CBDA and THCA. Within nine months, also thanks to the CBDA and THCA, I had also tapered off the injectable slow-release shot, both with no withdrawals AT ALL.

The programs were working. After eliminating the toxic root canals and broken infected teeth that were killing me slowly, I felt weightless. Compared to how the infection weighed me down, I felt like I lost 400 pounds from my head alone. Finally, free from overwhelming pain, I could attain the stability I needed to focus and put 100 percent of my energy into recovery.

There is a common misconception about what level of abstinence is needed to begin a journey of recovery. I didn't understand how to get off the addiction treadmill. I had struggled with addiction and mental health for so long that I needed help to create a safe and stable enough environment just to begin the journey of self-awareness that must precede the desire for recovery. I wonder if it is inhuman to expect a person to be 100 percent abstinent and free of any substance as a requirement to be accepted into a recovery program. Personally, I needed the in-between phases.

I knew a decade of heavy addiction burned into my sub-conscious demanded I do the real work to reprogram myself from the ground up. Once I experienced a taste of emotional intelligence (that wasn't about suppression of emotions) and meta-cognition, an awareness of my thoughts, I was disgusted with my previous ignorant perspective of mental health. As soon as I really understood and utilized the tools, I felt unstoppable. I now wielded a weapon against my addict-self that wasn't just abstinence from drugs or losing myself in full-time work.

Eventually, I was able to stop viewing myself as a victim, understanding that horrible events may have been inflicted on me by others, but it was my decisions that created my descent onto the dark path. By creating a state of accountability for my past choices, I empowered myself to make different decisions—to continue changing my life for the better. It most certainly was not easy or painless to give up my victim status and the accompanying resentment, but with my new understanding, I knew and found true freedom. As I learned from the Dharma Recovery Meditation of Equanimity, "I am not responsible for anyone else's happiness, nor is anyone else responsible for mine." Moments of realization like this freed me to focus on my path and to freely choose the direction I take for my one and only precious life.

In closing, so many synchronicities came together. There was no one moment of stepping into sobriety. The coincidences that set the stones for me to follow on my path to recovery were many. Such as a connection to staff members with the lived experience of addiction. Feeling heard and seen by someone who really understands. Inspired by those who have been there and modelled what was possible. To learn from each lesson and to avoid ruminating on the past. Continuing to make the needed changes day-by-day, such as ignoring the voice of my addict-self and listening to the voice of my sober-self long enough to make it stronger and louder. Both resided in me and still do. I kept showing up and engaging in support groups (the well-established ones as well as the new ones designed to meet the needs of the generations of today). All of this and more created a drive to keep on pushing myself. Encouraged further by Maverick staff, a spark ignited in me to pay it forward and created the job I do today as a Recovery Support Worker. In this capacity, I am privileged to lead a Dharma Recovery group, as well as many others. In the addiction services field, whatever job description we are given, we are a team; we keep the fires of recovery-thinking burning. This is what we do.

My foundational philosophy is that it takes dedication to change and a village of peers for true recovery. If you are on the recovery path—share what you're learning. This accelerates your progress more than anything else. I firmly believe you don't need 10 years of sobriety to assist someone else on their journey.

You only need to be two steps ahead and keep on walking. I'm living proof.

https://linktr.ee/taylorpridy

Saving My Son

by Teena Clipston

I've been here before. Never did I think I would be back again. But there I stood in the marina, with the fresh, salty air breezing across my skin and the autumn sun enveloping me. The boats reminded me of my old sailboat; yes, I have sailed through here before on my way to somewhere else. But I've been here, in this harbour city, even before then, and I have never spoken about it to anyone. Not since what happened, happened that day about twenty years ago.

I checked over my shoulder. Would he recognize me after all this time? *Of course he would*, I thought. I haven't changed much. I scanned the people walking by. Would I recognize him? Is that him? Is he still here in this town? My chest tightened… suddenly, it felt hard to breathe. What the hell was I doing back here? After all this time, I thought I was fine, but I wasn't. Everywhere I looked, I saw his face; he was watching me… and he was going to make good on his promise to kill me.

In an old red SUV, we had travelled across Canada, from Montreal to Nanaimo. I spent every moment of that trip trying to keep an insane person sane so he would not hurt me or my children. For the sake of this story, I will call him Stan.

The voices in Stan's head would tell him what he needed to do. And he was convinced we needed to get as far away from Montreal as possible.

I looked out the window across the endless flatness as we crossed the prairies. "You are going to do what I say; you're going to do what I fucking say," he rambled on. "Look at me!" He ordered. I turned my head from the window and looked towards him as he pulled a gun from under the seat, reminding me it was there. It looked like a snubnose .38-caliber revolver. He knows it will keep me in line.

"I hear you," I murmured, looking into the back seat and seeing my three young children asleep. I then reassured him, "Everything will be okay; once we get to the West Coast, we won't have to worry about Montreal anymore. You don't need to worry; I'm *not* going to leave you," I said while planning my escape.

Stan was the father of my youngest child, two years old at the time, and stepfather to my son, eight, and his sister, seven years old. The birth father of the two oldest siblings deserted them long ago for a cocaine addiction, which was more important than keeping food in the fridge or just showing up. I was a fool: young, naïve, with no particularly good guidance to follow. Diminished by childhood trauma, I just wanted a family and love. I definitely made mistakes. Stan was one, but from him, I was gifted the most beautiful soul of a child. So even in mistakes, good can blossom.

My son, Andrew, was now 28. I hadn't heard from him since he and his girlfriend broke up. He didn't want me to know what kind of mess he was in.

The small ferry arrived. I climbed aboard with my suitcases to jet across the harbour to a small Gulf Island across from Nanaimo where I would make a new home. It would be here where my son and I would come full circle with our trauma and healing. I just didn't know it yet.

The first few weeks of my return to the Nanaimo area—a place I had once fled—were filled with anxiety and paranoia. Each time I entered a grocery store, a pharmacy, or just walked down a street, I felt unsafe. Yet I convinced myself that Stan was long gone by now, and I didn't talk about the incident to anyone. Admitting that I had been in an abusive relationship would show weakness, stupidity, shame, and, worst of all, it would acknowledge the trauma that my children and I had endured. If I just push it away, put it out of my mind, just not speak about it, it will *go away. After all, my children were so young. They don't remember.*

But I was wrong.

I had learned to keep my head down back then, to avert my eyes from people. "Are you looking at that guy?" Stan would accuse me. His uncontrollable jealousy and delusions persisted through everyday simple tasks. I couldn't speak to anyone. I couldn't look at anyone. I walked on eggshells, waiting for his next rage event. Pretending for my children that everything was alright, even though I was terrified. Abusive relationships do not happen suddenly; they creep in, slowly controlling one thing then another, gradually escalating, until you are trapped. To make things worse, Stan had schizophrenia. He had been on medication for it, and suddenly decided to stop taking it.

Stan was a heavy drinker. Years before we had met, he had blacked out behind the wheel and smashed his pickup into a tree. He went flying through the windshield, headfirst, slamming his skull against the timber, resulting in the brain injury.

Why didn't I run? Because he held my youngest child hostage, I could not leave without her. I had to wait for the right moment to run—I needed all three of my kids with me. Why didn't I ask for help? Why didn't I say anything to my family or sister? My fear went beyond his bouts of rage; I knew he was capable of murder. I believed he would use that gun to kill us all. All my efforts went into keeping him calm long enough to figure out how to get me and my kids safely away.

Weeks passed.

I had managed to keep Stan calm for the most part. Pretending all was well. I kept my head down. My mouth shut. I cooked dinners. I never argued. Because of my obedience, he would let down his guard; he let me grocery shop on my own. Keeping my youngest, of course, a prisoner to make sure I would return. Each time I went to the store, I would hide a bit of money for my escape. To everyone on the outside, everything looked normal.

Until the calm broke.

His fist flew through the gyprock wall, destroying and raging. Furniture flew. Things came crashing down. The kids were crying; my son was screaming, "Stop it, stop it, stop it."

"Hide!" I yelled to them as Stan grabbed me by the hair and pulled me down on the bed, punching me. But they didn't hide. The door to the kids' room—opposite of mine—ajar, as they huddled together, screaming and crying for Stan to stop hurting their mom. I could see them from the corner of my eye. There was nothing I could do to protect them.

"You fucking whore," Stan yelled, oblivious to the children. He raged. "You were talking to someone, weren't you?! You think you're going to leave me! You are going to die before you leave me!"

I started to hyperventilate. "Please stop," I begged. "I'm not going to leave you," I said between gulps of air.

"Mommy," my son yelled. But Stan didn't stop. His large hands clasped around my neck. Tightening until I couldn't breathe. Suddenly, there was silence. All I heard was the sound of cracking as he squeezed the vertebrae in my neck. I looked at the kids, tears running down their faces, eyes wide in shock, helplessly staring at me being strangled, at me dying.

Then everything went dark.

I don't know how long I was out. I don't know what happened during that time. When I went unconscious and limp, he must have stopped—just short of choking me to death. The house was eerily quiet when I started to breathe again. Stan was gone.

When he returned, everything went back to being calm. Traumatized, pretending everything was normal—I knew my time was running out; we had to get out.

I kept my head down. I didn't speak to anyone. I cooked dinners. I smiled like everything was okay.

Weeks turned into months.

A day came when I sensed a calm. I took a risk. I steadied my voice, "You had such a hard day." I took a breath. "Why don't you let me take the kids grocery shopping to give you some relax-time? I will pick up some cold beer and steak and make you a nice dinner."

He looked at me. It was the longest thirty seconds of my life.

Suddenly, he dug into his pocket and pulled out the SUV keys, throwing them in the air across the room. I watched them fly towards me, almost in a surreal way. I snatched them out of the air. My heart pounding... I had waited for this moment.

"Come on, kids, let's go shopping," I said.

"Yay," they shouted.

We went to the police. I told my story. They escorted us to a women's shelter. The police could only hold Stan for 24 hours. He would then be released until his court date. We would need to leave town. They would relocate us to a Kelowna women's shelter for our safety.

The Kelowna women's shelter was a safe haven until I was back on my feet. They helped me navigate the system, obtain emergency welfare, and gather the things I needed to start over. I, in turn, volunteered to be in a commercial they were creating for domestic abuse and violence against women. I told my story on camera, with my face hidden.

Although they offered trauma support, I don't think I had the capacity to understand the damage trauma causes in the long-term for me or my children. My plan was to put it behind us and start over. And that is exactly what I did. I became a highly successful businesswoman in both the music industry and magazine publishing. I held my head up high and was not afraid to speak or be who I wanted to be. I was resilient. I was a creator who could do anything I put my mind to.

But I failed at one thing, and that was recognizing that my children may not have been as resilient as I was. At least my son wasn't. His inability to protect his mother when he was just a boy would eat away at his confidence. His own father deserting him when he was four years old would leave him feeling abandoned. And me being so busy with my career left him wanting to fill an emptiness we both did not yet understand.

My Son is Dying
I received a call from a dear woman at the Vernon Homeless Outreach Team, "Your son needs you. I don't think he has long left. He doesn't look good."

My son had overdosed several times and had severe infections all over his body.

Fentanyl was killing him.

I sat on my doorstep, crying, my cell phone clutched in my hand. Memories of him as a child passed through my mind. The image of him as a toddler with hands reaching, "Up mommy, up mommy," he would often say for me to pick him up and carry him. Then came dark clouds of guilt. *This is my fault. I was so stupid. So naïve. My son is broken. It's my fault.* I had to gather the strength to overcome my guilt.

I managed to get to Kelowna. (I had no car at that time.) Upon arrival, I called the outreach worker; she generously and bravely offered to drive my son, who was completely high and out of his mind, from Vernon to Kelowna, where I had rented a motel.

There was a knock at the door; my heart raced. I was afraid, I was happy, I was sad, I was everything all at once. There he stood, my boy, broken. He didn't look like him. He looked like one of those people you see on the street, that you walk by and pretend don't exist. His hair was long and wild; he had a scruffy beard that hid most of his face. His clothes were mismatched, ripped, and dirty. He was covered in black grime, which would turn out to be the soot of burned fentanyl on tinfoil, which covered his hands and left prints on everything he touched; I don't know when he last showered. Hidden under all of that was a thin skeleton of a man, covered in large open sores and in pain.

He collapsed onto the bed in a fetal position, sobbing. "Mom, I am so sorry," he cried over and over.

"It's okay." I hugged him. "I am here now." *I can do this; I can save my son.* I naively thought, *in a few weeks, he will be back to himself.*

He confided to me that his addiction started with prescription opioids for a rotten molar that had become infected and was causing him unbearable pain. These pills not only took his physical pain away, but he discovered they would also numb his emotional pain. He was not informed or aware of their addictive properties until it was too late. Once these pills were gone, he turned to the street to fill the need.

The first challenge that I faced was that my son was so completely addicted to fentanyl that he could not function without using every three or so hours. I learned quickly the devastating symptoms of withdrawal and the physical pain associated with it. For those who think one can just stop using opioids, it is nearly impossible, especially when your body is dependent on such a high dose. My son described the withdrawal as torture, where every bone in his body screamed out in pain. The solution, I thought, would be simple. We would get him on the OAT program (Opioid Agonist Treatment) with Interior Health. Not so simple. Getting an appointment with a doctor who could prescribe methadone was not easy. We were turned away several times. The system was overwhelmed, and not enough doctors were available.

Watching my son go into horrible withdrawal after withdrawal, I was left with no choice—I had to buy my son fentanyl. I had to walk the streets with him, amongst the homeless and addicts, looking for dealers, then sit with them amongst clouds of fentanyl smoke. Don't think I wasn't afraid. I was terrified.

I called the OAT clinic daily, only to be told there were no available appointments. We even took a cab from the motel to the clinic to see if we could get a doctor to write a prescription, only to be turned away. I was exhausted, worn down, angry, and felt hopeless. But determined.

It would get worse.

It was another day of walking up to the counter and being told there was no room for my son. Except this time, the lady behind the counter gave my son a paper bag. "What is that?" I asked him.

"Harm reduction bag," my son replied. Being new to all of this, I assumed that meant vitamins, medicines, peroxide, and band-aids… A harm reduction bag is not a first aid kit.

I left my son alone in the motel to go to the grocery store. Only to return to him unresponsive in the bathroom, sitting on the toilet with a needle in his arm. The harm reduction supply bag contained syringes, sterile water vials, stericups (cookers), alcohol swabs, and tourniquets. I hadn't seen him use a needle before. I was terrified that he was dead. "Andrew," I screamed, pulling the needle from his arm and tossing it into the sink. "Andrew. Wake up," I shook him.

How dangerous it was for the clinic not to tell me what was in that bag! How dangerous it was for them not to give me a naloxone kit and teach me how to use it! How dangerous it was for them to keep turning us away!

How dangerous it was for my son to hide it all from me! I was angry and looked to place the blame on someone somewhere.

He was still breathing. Slowly. "Come on, Andrew, please wake up," I begged. He stirred. Moving slowly like a drunken person.

"Mommmmm," he slurred. "I'mmmmm ooooookkkk." He could barely talk. I moved him from the toilet to the bed, where I watched him breathe for the next couple of hours. In the same way you would check on a newborn baby, I watched his chest move up and down. Until he woke up, needing to use again.

Again, we returned to the clinic. This time, I refused to leave. I threatened. "If you don't get my son in to see a doctor, I am calling the media." A doctor appeared within 15 minutes to see us.

It came time to find a way to get back home with my son. The doctor prescribed my son enough sedatives and opioids to keep him sleeping for the eight-hour drive to Vancouver Island. It cost me $1000 to hire a driver to take us. There was no way my son could have flown.

I put my son up in a cabin in my backyard. He was quiet, full of shame, and wanted to hide himself from the world. He did not want to speak about his feelings. But even without words, I could see his mental anguish and the pain in his eyes. Everyday, until he was strong enough to get up, I sat next to him. I brought him food. And told him everything was going to be alright. And every night, I worried he would die in his sleep. The pain of opioid withdrawal was horrific. But he was also ill, with countless infections, malnutrition, and depression. Later, a blood test confirmed that he was also fighting a severe hepatitis C infection.

It was like watching someone die. Sweat covered his face, pale and distorted in agony. His thin body shivered, unable to move. I did what I could, without a medical degree, without knowing anything really about what he was going through. I wished I could have taken both his physical pain and mental anguish away. And so, as any mother would do, I took care of my sick child. I made soup, I put a cloth on his head, and I ran to the cannabis store to buy him CBD/THC gummies to help him sleep. I watched him day in and day out. I educated myself on addiction. I sat by his bedside reading *In the Realm of Hungry Ghosts* by Dr. Gabor Maté, beginning to understand the trauma behind addiction. There was no denying what happened over twenty years ago contributed in part to my son's emptiness.

"Do you remember what happened?" I asked him.

"I remember everything." His next words were tortured. "Do you know how I felt, not being able to protect my own mom?" His eyes teared up, and he looked away. He was filled with guilt.

Many days of sitting and watching my son in withdrawal would pass. Little did I know, worrying about him dying was the easy part. A roller coaster of hell ensued.

There is no straight line to recovery. *Did I really think I could save my son from a fentanyl addiction in just a few weeks?*

The first six months into his recovery were unbearable. He battled with psychosis and spent hours speaking to entities I could not see. He said there were black, shadowy figures in the trees watching him. And as I stood in front of him one day, speaking, he told me to stop morphing into someone else. "You're not my mom," he fearfully said. "Stop changing your face." *What if he tried to hurt me*, I thought? I stepped back from him. *Frightened, my son's psychosis reminded me of Stan's delusions and the voices he spoke to.*

He disappeared on occasion, lost in the streets, sometimes for days, and return in some kind of mess. Sometimes beaten, always robbed, and sometimes without any recollection at all. "You don't understand the pain I am in," he howled.

He was right. I did not understand the pain he was in. He was also unable to convey that pain in any other way except by harming himself and destroying his life. He did not want to talk about the trauma or his feelings.

I never knew from one day to the next if he would be overdosing on fentanyl, up for days on meth in psychosis, sleeping for days on benzos, or sick because of some poisonous concoction. The drugs from the street were contaminated. You never knew what was in them. Each drug meant dealing with a new personality. Each day passed, with me thinking this would be the day he would die of an overdose. I kept preparing myself mentally for finding him dead. The wonder woman I thought I was—capable of saving my son—was about to crumble.

It didn't happen overnight; it was slow, like stones being placed onto my back, one by one weighing me down, until I would buckle into pieces. It strangled my self-worth and pulled me down to a vibrational level left for dark things. I sometimes wondered if those entities my son spoke to in psychosis were real. Were there demons preying on addicts? I felt the energy around me change. I could not escape it. After six months, my son's addiction was breaking me. I wasn't as strong as I thought. Suddenly, I felt trapped again. *How do I fix this? What do I do? Where can I find help? There is no one coming.* Those were the thoughts that caught my breath, tightened my chest, and made me feel like there was no escaping this hell. The dark energy of my son's addiction was choking me.

I lowered my head in shame; I was afraid to speak, and the floor became eggshells again.

I didn't know what to do. It was then that I understood why there were so many young people on the streets, stuck in their addictions and exiled from their families. Taking care of someone with substance abuse disorder is unbelievably difficult. You sacrifice your life and descend into a 24/7 darkness full of sorrow and chaos. That, in itself, is traumatizing and most definitely causes post-traumatic stress disorder. And that is what was happening to me. I was being traumatized all over again.

I needed help—just someone to spend time with him so I could take a break and maybe get some sleep. Someone to run errands or someone to take him out of the house for a bit so I could work in peace. I hadn't slept for days. Actually, I hadn't slept properly in months. I could feel the stress in my body causing illness. I had digestive issues, allergies, tight and sore muscles, lack of concentration, fatigue, anxiety, panic attacks, depression, and was filled with hopelessness. Every time I reached out, the advice was the same: tough love. '*Kick him to the street.*' I knew this would kill him, but at the same time, I knew the stress was killing me.

Add shame to this. Some of my neighbours showed compassion, but others made it clear my son was not welcome in our neighbourhood.

I kept my head down; I didn't speak to anyone; I cooked dinners, and I smiled like everything was okay.

Weeks passed.

Until I just could not take it anymore.

I was exhausted. I was feeling hopeless. I didn't see a way out of my situation. My son was so completely oblivious to what I was going through. Trapped in his own prison, until he witnessed me falling apart. A rant about how he needed money triggered me.

I fell to the floor, sobbing; I couldn't catch my breath. I gasped for air. The room spun. Between short breaths, I begged, "God, please, I can't do this anymore… I can't, I can't do this anymore." My son, confused, did not know how to react.

Then, realizing he had to help me, he reached out to pull me off the floor. "It's okay, mom. I'm going to stop. I will get better. I promise." Words he hoped would comfort me. "I promise, Mom, I am so sorry. I promise."

This was the moment things changed. He pulled me up from the floor.

When I finally caught my breath, I spoke, "This can't be my life, this can't be your life… do you understand? There is so much in this world; you need to see it. You need to see the beauty in this world because this, what we are living right now, is not life… I want my life back," I said firmly.

I then examined myself and how much I was destroyed. I needed my strength back. I had lost control of my life. I needed *me* back. That woman who could manifest the most beautiful life, where was she?

I needed to heal.

I needed to get rid of that dark energy that enveloped me and was trying to pull me down.

I prayed to God.

I changed my viewpoint.

I took care of myself.

I loved my son so much that evil didn't stand a chance.

"You have the power to recreate your life," I said to him. "You deserve a beautiful life."

I accepted that addiction was a form of self-harm rooted in trauma and perpetuated by the pain of not loving oneself—actually hating oneself. It is becoming the victim of all the terrible words that were ever said to you, all the terrible things that were ever done to you, all the terrible things you witnessed, then manifesting all that into what you think you deserve. It is guilt; it is shame; it is rooted in not understanding why terrible things happen and having meaning in life. It is Godless.

Forgive yourself.

I kept telling him how he was worthy. How the situation he was in was not his fault. I talked about what happened when he was a child and how Stan was to blame and not him. I tried to remove the guilt he felt and empower him with possibilities.

"Imagine a circle," I explained to him, "and in that circle is your environment. In it, there is constant chaos, poverty, loneliness, struggle, pain, drugs, alcohol, other broken people, and no vision of anything else. What if being in that circle made you believe there was nothing outside of it?"

Outside of that circle is healing and hope.

"There is a whole other world waiting for you; you just can't see it yet." I said, "You can create whatever you want in your life. You just need to envision it and believe in it. Have faith. Heal from the past, find beauty in things today, and let that lead you to a better tomorrow."

I was going to show him that there was beauty in this world and that life was worth living. I was going to give him hope so he would want something better for himself. I decided we'd take seven trips in seven months to see the beauty around us. And we did.

I also took time to heal myself, making myself and my life a priority.

Part of my healing was to examine my motives carefully. I was attached to an outcome that I wanted to achieve; I wanted to save my son. Would that make me a hero in my story? Would that alleviate my guilt? Was it a self-conquest that I needed to win? Was I trying to control his life, was I overbearing, and God forbid, was I enabling? Or was I simply trying to take his pain away by showing him that he was worthy of love and a good life? I focused on healing myself. Understanding my own trauma. Understanding my childhood and all the things that followed and led to where I am now. The work that needed to be done would ultimately be on the inside, not the outside.

Not suddenly, but slowly, I could see him change. And I could definitely see a change in me.

Andrew went on the rehab waitlist for Edgewood Treatment Centre in Nanaimo. The waitlist was long; it would be eight months before his admission. It was not an easy thing for him to do; he was afraid to leave me alone, fearing something would happen to me, but he did it and successfully completed the program. He finally had a vision for something else.

My son has completely transformed from that person I rescued from the street back to who he is meant to be. He looks good. He is handsome. He is no longer sick. His mind is sharp and back to normal. His self-loathing and shame have dissipated.

Almost a year after being discharged from rehab, we stood watching the sunset on Hornby Island; the sun's rays cast amazing colours against the water, the sailboats creating beautiful silhouettes against the sky. There was beauty in life. We laughed, talked, and shared ideas on what was next for him and for me. I see in my son a confidence—he now knows he can create the life he so deserves.

I stood there, smiling. I stepped closer. And realized I saved my son.

Unconditional love is needed to pull anyone out of darkness. We have the capacity to love as parents, friends, relatives, and neighbours. The smallest gesture, a smile, a word of acknowledgement, imparts love.

Hope is given through the idea of possibilities. A glimpse, a sharing, a picture, a story, a shared experience that provides a preview into the world beyond pain and addiction. I learned to do this with my son. Step into the world of possibilities—and show those who are suffering those possibilities, which empowers them to help themselves.

From there, you will find healing and hope.

Community Letters

We would like to express our heartfelt gratitude to our sponsors and supporters, whose contributions made this book possible. Their commitment and belief in our mission have helped us bring these stories to life. The following community letters are from them, offering not only their support but also valuable resources for those seeking help with addiction recovery, personal messages of hope, and more. Their generosity extends beyond these pages, touching the lives of many on their healing journeys.

THE CORE CENTRE OF HEALTH

Dear Reader,

I am writing to express my heartfelt support for this book and to commend the incredible work that you have all done in addressing the important and sensitive topic of addiction and recovery.

As someone who recognizes the challenges that individuals and families face in navigating addiction, your book serves as a powerful beacon of hope and a valuable resource for the community.

The insightful approach to addiction, grounded in both personal experiences and a deep understanding of the complexities of recovery, offers a compassionate and honest perspective that resonates with readers from all walks of life. By sharing these stories, you not only break down the stigma surrounding addiction but also offer a roadmap for healing and transformation.

This book is much more than a collection of memoirs or an educational text; it is a lifeline for those who are struggling with addiction, as well as for their loved ones. The raw vulnerability with which each author shares their journey brings a sense of authenticity that is rare and refreshing in this field. It reminds readers that recovery is not a straight path but rather a series of steps, setbacks, and triumphs that require resilience and community support.

I believe that *this* book has the potential to make a profound impact on individuals, families, and communities affected by addiction. The courage to tell these stories and the dedication to helping others find a way forward is truly inspiring. It is my hope that this book will continue to reach more people, offering them the support, knowledge, and inspiration needed to overcome their own battles.

Thank you for your invaluable contribution to the conversation on addiction and recovery. This work is not only timely but necessary, and it will undoubtedly continue to touch lives and foster healing in profound ways.

With sincere appreciation and support,

Dr. Troy Tater
https://thecorekelowna.com/

ASK WELLNESS SOCIETY

Dear Reader,

ASK Wellness Society was originally initiated in response to a health crisis flooded with stigma and a sense of hopeless despair. Founded in 1992 as the AIDS Society of Kamloops, the Society was formed to promote health and wellness and to provide education to strengthen the Kamloops community. We aimed to provide hope for individuals in what often felt like the most hopeless of situations. Fast-forward to over thirty years later, where we have adapted our services and changed our name, but continue offering the same hope for different destructive and threatening crises. Across the province, the impacts of the toxic drug supply are demonstrated all too frequently, with no one demographic being immune to the risks or the consequences of addictions. The intersection of this public health emergency and the growing number of affordable housing casualties, paired with our inability to hold people accountable for criminal activity, has left the province, and the country, with a tsunami of social and health impacts.

Our vision is to work towards a society that recognizes the value and potential of all individuals. This requires acceptance of the choices that individuals make and an acknowledgement of the disproportionate impact of harm on certain groups due to individual and cultural realities. We are client-centred, providing services and support in an interactive manner that is responsive to individual and collective needs. We are focused on developing prevention goals and strategies that support a holistic approach to health, with offices throughout the BC Interior in Kamloops, Merritt, and Penticton.

When providing supports and solutions, we look at substance use through the lens of the Four Pillar Approach model, looking at the resources of Prevention (early intervention, education), Harm Reduction (reducing as best as possible the most severe impacts of substance use), Treatment/Recovery (options to treat substance use disorders effectively, promptly, and universally), and Enforcement (incarceration, judicial orders for those who commit offences related to addictions). We provide programs across a continuum from streets to homes to health to employment, and the following services offer support for substance use, aiming to create formal pathways between harm reduction services and recovery.

- **Street Outreach and Overdose Prevention:** In Kamloops and Merritt, this program serves as a first point of contact for those facing homelessness or anybody who is affected by substance use and does not know where to turn. Through these services, we connect community members in need with health and housing resources. The program works to deliver safe and effective harm reduction services to individuals while mitigating the impact of homelessness and addiction on community members and business partners.

- **Naloxone Training:** In Kamloops, we have trained hundreds of our fellow community members on how to provide life-saving naloxone in case of an opioid overdose. Hands-on training is offered in one-to-one or group settings at our site or at your location.

- **Drug Checking:** In Kamloops, Merritt, and Penticton, the Community Drug Checking Service, in partnership with Interior Health Authority (IHA) and the BC Centre for Substance Use, allows free testing of substance samples that is both fast and anonymous. The service makes use of the Fourier Transform Infrared Spectroscopy (FTIR) to analyze and identify components within substances to increase awareness for individuals who use. Samples are taken and continue to lead to immediate drug alerts sent out by the Interior Health Authority. These alerts are designed to reduce the immediate risk to individuals using substances and mitigate the continued rise of overdose rates across the province.

- **Maverick Supportive Recovery and Career Development Centre:** Based in Kamloops, the 42-bed program provides opportunities for people who are wanting to tackle their addictions and other barriers in a safe and supportive setting. Through funding from the Ministry of Mental Health and Addictions, the Interior Health Authority, BC Housing, and others, the Society can offer a three-phase supportive recovery long-term living environment that allows people of all genders to tackle their addictions and access and maintain employment. Participants are provided with individual-based supports, including substance use treatment, relapse prevention planning, life skills support, addictions counselling, peer coaching, and career development opportunities. This three-prong approach transitions individuals from support through early recovery, to stabilization, and finally to employment and education support for the successful transition into independent living.

- **Health Education:** In Kamloops, we have a team of qualified staff to help participants improve their health. Whether it be to assist in finding a doctor or to transport individuals out of town for specialist appointments, the team can help and provide hope. Through this service, we create a common purpose of building capacity to positively impact the quality of life of individuals living with complex health needs. We also provide needle harm reduction supplies at all our locations and housing facilities. The Health Educator provides medical advocacy, health counselling, connections to treatment, education about treatment and disorders, transportation to medical appointments, and referrals to services we are unable to provide. This is the only HIV/Hep C community-based program in Kamloops and has a focus on reducing stigma and providing education.

- **Snṗaʔx̌tantn:** Based in Penticton, this 54-unit building offers recovery-focused supportive housing. Offering affordable, accessible studio apartments within a four-story building, the unique program at Snṗaʔx̌tantn will also provide in-house access to substance use recovery counselling, Indigenous cultural supports, and vocational support.

Along with our original values of Hope, Inclusion, Compassion, and Trust, we added a fifth value of Adaptation in 2022. In order to meet the needs of the communities we serve, we are ever-evolving in the services we provide. For current programming offered, please go to www.askwellness.ca or email info@askwellness.ca for more information.

Sincerely,
Bob Hughes, Executive Officer
www.askwellness.ca

Community Letter

JOHN HOWARD SOCIETY OF BRITISH COLUMBIA

Dear Reader,

For over 90 years, the John Howard Society of British Columbia, or JHSBC, has championed better options for people who experience social injustice or are involved in the criminal justice system. Working directly and with a network of regional John Howard Societies across BC, John Howards in BC provide supports for people in need and a trusted, balanced voice for policy and program reform. We take an integrative approach, centering around the individualized and unique needs of the people we serve and working in collaboration with a range of community partners.

It will be no secret to readers of *Healing Mind, Body and Soul* that social injustice has its roots in many self-perpetuating and interconnected causes—lack of affordable and accessible housing, barriers to educational opportunities, colonialism and the residential school tragedy, trauma and victimization, poverty, barriers to employment, inadequate access to health and mental health care, stigma, and gaps in community connection and inclusion. Not the least among these, and at the heart of this book, is addiction, the prejudice and social stigma attached to it, and the profound deficit in supports for people who experience it. We want to emphasize three aspects of this particular multi-dimensional challenge.

First, JHSBC recognizes that addiction is a matter of health and wellbeing not a criminal act. Criminalization of people who experience addiction is not an appropriate or effective way to address it. While addiction is more prevalent among people who are marginalized, it affects people from all walks of life. How many of us don't know someone whose life has been affected by addiction? Even so, social attitudes toward people who experience addiction force them to hide, deter them from being open to the help that may be available, and, at worst, put them at risk of using alone without the support they need in the event of an overdose. As a community, we owe it to ourselves to learn how we can better accept and support people who experience addiction, rather than exclude them.

Second, JHSBC believes that governments can and must do more. In July 2024, there were still more than six deaths per day due to the poisoned and unregulated drug supply in British Columbia. The John Howard Societies of BC and Okanagan-Kootenay had the privilege of jointly addressing British Columbia's Select Standing Committee on Health in the summer of 2022. Many of our recommendations from then still stand. We ask the government to adopt and publish explicit and measurable short-, medium-, and long-term targets and commitments, and that they report progress frequently and publicly. What gets measured and monitored gets done. The times also call for political courage not to back away from innovative measures to improve safe supply, safe use, and decriminalization. And why not dare to be visionary—commit publicly that no one who asks for mental health and substance use help will wait longer than a day and take the action needed to make it happen.

Third, and fundamentally related to the message in this book, JHSBC recognizes the crucial contribution of people with lived experience as a source of inspiration and as a source of support for those who are on their journey to recovery. The stories of people with lived experience provide hope and show that healing and recovery is possible. As a source of direct support, people with lived experience can provide peer to peer help without judgment or hierarchy, facilitate learning through shared experience, and share a positive focus on wellbeing and recovery.

For more about JHSBC and John Howard Societies in Victoria, North Island, Okanagan – Kootenay and Northern BC please visit https://johnhowardbc.ca/.

Sincerely,
Mark Medgyesi,
Executive Director, John Howard Society of BC

ALBERTA ADOLESCENT RECOVERY CENTRE

Dear Reader,

My son is alive today due to compassionate intervention at the age of 17. Amidst multiple stays at mental health units, group homes, a court-ordered stay at a safe house, and multiple overdoses, addiction took control of his and our lives. In the two weeks before entering long-term treatment, our hearts said goodbye to him twice as he was resuscitated and placed on life support. His addiction had made him a danger to himself. The pain of sitting by his bedside felt unbearable. I could not save my son. There was no doubt that we had reached a point where he could no longer make decisions to keep himself safe. After years of daily all-consuming worry and unpredictability, we finally discovered that parent intervention was an option.

It is hard to understand the anguish of this journey and this decision until you love someone who struggles with addiction. It took its toll on every member of our family unit. It should never have come to this. The loneliness and fear of judgment along this journey are bringing families to their knees daily. Ours is just one of many stories of hundreds of families I have met through treatment at the Alberta Adolescent Recovery Centre (AARC) who have struggled to find treatment at this level. I have been blessed to connect with a powerful community of families who have been united by the challenges of youth addiction. For many of us, intervention was the solution. It gave us hope in a way we never felt possible on the desperate days of this journey when we could not find our next step. It has, without any doubt, saved our son and, in turn, our family, as we never would have recovered from losing him. Treatment provided a space where it was safe for my son to be vulnerable with his pain and, in turn, to recover from his addiction with dignity, something I believe everyone deserves. Today, we proudly watch him prioritise his recovery and focus on becoming the healthiest version of himself.

I feel it is important to share our journey of hope to raise awareness in our communities around available treatment for youth addiction. This is not just about reaching youth who are struggling with addiction. It is also about recognizing the impact on parents, siblings, loved ones, friends, and advocates who may be carrying the weight and worry of this journey while being viewed by society as a moral failure. Judgment and shame should play no part as distressed families navigate treatment options. Anyone dealing with the impact of youth addiction deserves a community of hope and care.

Unfortunately, we are living in a drug culture, which means that there are many children within our communities who are chemically dependent. I believe that underneath the layers of challenging behaviours, there are underlying mental health concerns that need to be addressed. But, when severe substance abuse is the main concern, it cannot be ignored. It is only when the fog of the addiction has been lifted that these children can begin to work through their pain. As part of long-term treatment at the Alberta Adolescent Recovery Centre, my son was given time to remove the layer of addiction for a solid 8-10 months. This time allowed for a period of abstinence and provided space for him to consider navigating a different path, substance-free. At AARC, again under the expert care of psychiatry, psychology, clinical counselling, peer support, nursing, and nutritional and physical health specialists, youth are given the opportunity to put life on pause until they find themselves. Halfway through treatment, youth are reintegrated back into school while being continuously supported by the program. As parents during treatment, we opened our home to care for abstinent youth struggling like our own son. It was an intense and amazing experience, as we witnessed many young people work incredibly hard through the 12 steps of AA to heal from being so broken to finding purpose and direction.

Overriding my residual discomfort with sharing our journey, I feel strongly that it is time to remove the stigma from conversations surrounding youth addiction. Instead, I feel that openly supporting the next steps for families can play a more valuable role on this path. Conversations for family members around addiction are so difficult as they are filled with pain, shame, and guilt. De-stigmatizing adolescent addiction could make these conversations easier and shorten the journey of finding appropriate treatments when in crisis. We are blessed to have a community with a strong focus on mental health. My hope is that families of youth that cross the line into addiction are not left to deal with this additional terrifying layer alone. That is where supports become difficult to find but are needed the most. Families deserve to be able to make these decisions for their children who do not recognise that they need help.

Following treatment in 2022, I accepted the position as AARC's Community Outreach Specialist. I am honoured to work at an organization that does not hesitate to go the extra mile to help these kids when all seems hopeless. I can say, without any doubt, that my son is alive today due to the compassion-based care that he received through treatment at AARC. I am passionate about raising awareness around treatment options in the hope that other families can navigate and access supports in an easier way. Looking back, I can clearly see the difference it would have made for us to have access to supports or next steps at an earlier stage in our journey.

Today, as part of working at AARC, I see youth in treatment who have struggled for many reasons and have turned to substances to cope with their loneliness, only to find themselves in the grips of addiction. They work hard to find a way out of their pain and shame through the 12 steps of AA, which provide them with tools to navigate life in a way that they can change their path and access a substance-free life. As the majority of the staff at AARC are, themselves, graduates of the program, I see daily the effectiveness of the peer support component of the unique program. It is powerful to watch the connections that are made with other youth who have walked this journey and feel passionate about offering hope through giving back to new clients, all of whom enter the doors of AARC shattered and their families broken.

It has never been so important to raise awareness around youth addiction. Please share this message in the hope that we can make a positive difference towards saving our precious children's lives.

Ciara Brady
www.aarc.ab.ca

KI-LOW-NA FRIENDSHIP SOCIETY

Welcome to the Ki-Low-Na Friendship Society;

This year is the 50th Anniversary, of the 1974 opening of the Kelowna Friendship Society. The value of this organization to the community is felt by many of all ages, including those living with addiction. Social programs, cultural supports and services for those identifying as Indigenous peoples, are an important part and focus of all that is offered.

- **Mental Health and Wellness programs:** AA meetings, Drug and Alcohol Counselling, Wellbriety meetings, Healing and Wellness Circles, including Social and Culturally Focused Programs for men and woman.
- **Family Services:** Family Support, Roots, Supervised Access Visits, CAPC for children and parents, AIDP and ASCD infants and children supports and the Skemxist Preschool.
- **Disability Tax Aid:** free tax preparation for those living with disability (PWD) and others with multiple barriers, or low-income individuals. (for up to 10 years back)
- **Elders Program:** culturally appropriate, holistic approach, focuses on maintaining wellness through the balanced teachings of the medicine wheel. Services include assistance with obtaining health care and contact with the Aboriginal Patient Navigator, mental health services, housing, Canada Pension Plan, and Old Age Security. Activities include, monthly Elders Luncheons, Elders Picnics, medicine picking, yoga, Tai-Chi and other activities.

- **Reaching Home program:** the Kelowna Friendship Society has been designated with the management of the Government of Canada's Reaching Home Strategy, Indigenous funding within the Kelowna area, supplying support and guidance to the Indigenous Homeless Community Advisory Board, effectively administering sub-projects for numerous years.
    - With our many years of experience delivering frontline Outreach support services, we have consistently administered sub-projects under this funding initiative. Committed to excellence, community engagement and transparent stewardship, addressing Indigenous homelessness and advancing the wellbeing of our community members.
- **Annual Events and Opportunities for volunteering:** Turtle Island Festival, Truth and Reconciliation Day, Sisters in Spirit Walk, Community Family Nights.

Our History:
The Ki-Low-Na Friendship Society is one of over 100 Friendship Centres in Canada. We are a registered non-profit society, and donations are tax-deductible. The Friendship Centre Movement includes the National Association of Friendship Centres, provincial associations, and Friendship Centres throughout Canada.

We provide programs and services to all peoples in various life stages. We are always looking for volunteers to support many of our ongoing programs.

Check out the Ki-Low-Na Friendship Society listings, of our ongoing programs and services: www.kfs.bc.ca

Mission Statement:
The Ki-Low-Na Friendship Society will provide for the mental, emotional, physical and spiritual well-being of all peoples through the development of community-based services, while encouraging the community to preserve, share and promote Aboriginal cultural distinctiveness.

Memberships & Affiliations:
- British Columbia Association of Aboriginal Friendship Centres
- National Association of Friendship Centres
- Aboriginal Housing Management Association
- British Columbia Non-Profit Housing Association
- Canadian Housing and Renewal Association

- Partners in Community Collaboration (PICC)
- Journey Home

Friendship Centres provide culturally relevant programs and services for Indigenous people living in urban centres across Canada in multiple areas including, health, shelter, youth, justice and development. They have also become a place for Indigenous and non-Indigenous people to come together, to share traditions, and to learn from one another.

The Friendship Centre Movement—made up of over 100 Friendship Centres and seven Provincial/Territorial Associations—is the largest and most comprehensive urban Indigenous service delivery network in Canada. Their collective work reaches millions of points of contact in a year and hundreds of thousands of people every single day from coast-to-coast-to-coast.

Find out where your local Friendship Centre or Provincial/Territorial Association is located and consider volunteering and providing your time, resources or donate, to support them in continuing to provide crucial front-line work across Canada.

Learn more *about the National Association of Friendship Centres: https://nafc.ca/home*

From all of us here,

Ki-Low-Na Friendship Society
www.kfs.bc.ca

SENA COLLEGE OF MASSAGE THERAPY

To Whom It May Concern,

The Role of Massage Therapy in Addressing the Addiction Crisis
In response to the ongoing addiction crisis affecting so many individuals and communities, Sena is committed to supporting those struggling with addiction by highlighting the significant benefits of massage therapy.

Addiction is a deeply complex issue that impacts both the body and mind. We believe in a holistic approach to recovery, where addressing physical, emotional, and psychological well-being is essential. Massage therapy is a valuable complementary treatment that can ease the physical and emotional burdens of addiction recovery.

Massage therapy helps alleviate common physical symptoms experienced during recovery, such as muscle tension, pain, and withdrawal effects. It also promotes relaxation, reduces anxiety, and improves sleep patterns, which are often disrupted during recovery. Furthermore, therapeutic touch fosters a positive connection between the mind and body, encouraging a sense of well-being and self-care.

At Sena, we are dedicated to training massage therapists who are not only highly skilled but also compassionate and understanding of the unique challenges faced by individuals in recovery. Our specialized training programs equip our students to make a meaningful contribution to addiction treatment and recovery.

In conclusion, Sena stands with those affected by addiction and is committed to being part of the solution. We believe that massage therapy is a powerful tool in comprehensive addiction recovery, offering vital support to those on their healing journey. We appreciate the opportunity to support this project.

Sincerely,
Lindsey Sloan, RMT
Program Director
Sena College of Massage Therapy
www.senacollege.ca

Resources

The following list of addiction resources and rehabs has been compiled with the utmost care and attention to accuracy. While we strive to provide the most current and comprehensive information available, we acknowledge that there may be resources not included or updates that have occurred since this list was compiled. We encourage individuals seeking help to verify the details and consult additional sources to ensure they find the most appropriate support for their needs.

CANADA & USA: ADDICTION RECOVERY RESOURCES

Canada: Addiction Recovery Resources

Alcoholics Anonymous (AA) - Canada
- Website: www.aa.org
- A fellowship of individuals dedicated to helping each other achieve and maintain sobriety through regular meetings and support groups across Canada.

Narcotics Anonymous (NA) - Canada
- Website: www.na.org
- A peer-supported recovery network for individuals dealing with drug addiction, offering meetings and resources across Canada.

Healing and Hope for Families - Online Support Group
- Website: www.skool.com/shift-labs-1121
- A weekly Zoom meeting provides families with a supportive space to be seen, heard, and guided through the challenges of loving someone struggling with addiction. Led by experienced professionals, the group offers counseling and leadership facilitation to help families navigate these difficult situations.

Addiction Helpline - Alberta Health Services
- Website: www.albertahealthservices.ca
- A confidential service providing support, information, and referrals to Alberta residents struggling with addiction.

BC Alcohol and Drug Information and Referral Service
- Website: www.healthlinkbc.ca
- A 24-hour helpline providing information on addiction services and referrals to local treatment facilities.

BC Centre on Substance Use
- Website: www.bccsu.ca
- Offers research, education, and guidance on best practices in addiction treatment and harm reduction across British Columbia.

Luke Wiltshire Life Coach & Addictions Consultant
- Website: www.thelukewiltshire.com
- A Personal Development Mentor and Recovery Expert specializing in addiction consultation. Focused on helping individuals transition from intention to action, empowering them to take ownership of their life's direction and achieve meaningful change.

OATS (Opioid Agonist Therapy Support) Program
- Location: Multiple regions in British Columbia
- Website: www.interiorhealth.ca
- Provides opioid agonist therapy (OAT) with medications like methadone or Suboxone, counselling, and support for those managing opioid dependence.

Overdose Prevention Services (OPS) - BC
- Website: www.bccsu.ca
- Safe, supervised consumption spaces offering harm reduction supplies and support for individuals using substances.

Addictions Foundation of Manitoba
- Website: www.afm.mb.ca
- Offers public education, counselling, and a range of addiction recovery programs, including detox and residential services.

ConnexOntario
- Website: www.connexontario.ca

• Provides free, confidential information on mental health, addiction, and problem gambling services across Ontario.

Ontario Addiction Treatment Centres (OATC)
  • Website: www.oatc.ca
  • Specializes in opioid replacement therapy and counselling for individuals dealing with opioid addiction across multiple locations in Ontario.

USA: Addiction Recovery Resources

SAMHSA (Substance Abuse and Mental Health Services Administration) National Helpline
  • Website: www.samhsa.gov
  • A free, confidential, 24/7 helpline offering treatment referrals and information for individuals facing substance use disorders across the USA.

National Institute on Drug Abuse (NIDA)
  • Website: www.drugabuse.gov
  • Provides comprehensive research, educational materials, and resources for understanding and treating addiction.

California Department of Health Care Services – Substance Use Treatment Services
  • Website: www.dhcs.ca.gov
  • Provides information and resources for addiction treatment programs, harm reduction, and recovery services across California.

Partnership to End Addiction
  • Website: www.drugfree.org
  • Offers resources and personalized support for families dealing with addiction, including a helpline and online tools.

Connecticut Department of Mental Health and Addiction Services (DMHAS)
  • Website: www.portal.ct.gov
  • Provides comprehensive addiction and mental health services, including inpatient, outpatient, and community-based support.

Florida Department of Children and Families - Substance Abuse
  • Website: www.myflfamilies.com

- Offers statewide programs for addiction treatment and recovery, including prevention, detox, and rehab services.

Georgia Council on Substance Abuse
- Website: www.gasubstanceabuse.org
- A recovery community organization providing peer support, education, and advocacy for people recovering from addiction in Georgia.

Illinois Department of Human Services - Division of Substance Use Prevention and Recovery (SUPR)
- Website: www.dhs.state.il.us
- Offers addiction prevention, intervention, treatment, and recovery services throughout Illinois.

New Jersey Addiction Services Hotline
- Website: www.nj211.org
- A 24/7 confidential helpline connecting individuals with local addiction treatment and support services across New Jersey.

Pennsylvania Department of Drug and Alcohol Programs (DDAP)
- Website: www.ddap.pa.gov
- Provides addiction prevention, intervention, treatment, and recovery resources across Pennsylvania, including local rehab centers.

Tennessee REDLINE
- Website: www.taadas.org/redline
- A 24/7 addiction and mental health helpline providing referrals to treatment facilities and support services across Tennessee.

Texas Health and Human Services - Substance Use Services
- Website: www.hhs.texas.gov
- Offers resources for substance use treatment, including detox, counseling, and inpatient rehabilitation services across Texas.

CANADA & USA: REHAB CENTRES

Canadian Drug Rehab Centres Directory
- Website: www.canadiandrugrehabcentres.com
- A comprehensive directory of rehab facilities and addiction treatment services in Canada.

SAMHSA's Treatment Locator (USA)
- Website: www.findtreatment.samhsa.gov
- Searchable directory of addiction and mental health treatment centers across the USA.

Canada: Rehab Centres

ASK Wellness Society
- Location: Kamloops, British Columbia
- Website: www.askwellness.ca
- Offers community-focused support services for those dealing with addiction, including housing and harm reduction.

Cedars at Cobble Hill
- Location: Cobble Hill, British Columbia
- Website: www.cedarscobblehill.com
- Comprehensive inpatient and outpatient addiction treatment with family programs and a focus on long-term recovery.

Edgewood Treatment Centre
- Location: Nanaimo, British Columbia
- Website: www.edgewoodhealthnetwork.com
- A well-known rehab center offering comprehensive inpatient treatment for substance use disorders.

Freedom's Door
- Location: Kelowna, British Columbia
- Website: www.freedomsdoorkelowna.com
- Provides Christian-based residential treatment for men struggling with addiction.

Hemi House
- Location: Kelowna, British Columbia
- Website: www.hemishealingcentre.com
- Hemi House is part of Hemi's Healing Centre, a non-profit organization offering sober living recovery programs specifically for women, including those who are self-identifying, 2SLGBTQ+, and from marginalized communities. The centre provides a holistic approach to addiction recovery, focusing on therapies like art, yoga, and Indigenous healing rituals. Programs aim to support long-term recovery through personalized care, mental health services, and outreach.

John Howard Society of British Columbia
- Location: Various locations across British Columbia
- Website: www.johnhowardbc.ca
- Provides services related to addiction recovery, mental health, and reintegration into society, including transitional housing and counseling.

Ki-Low-Na Friendship Society
- Location: Kelowna, British Columbia
- Website: www.kfs.bc.ca
- Offers addiction treatment and wellness programs tailored to Indigenous communities, focusing on holistic healing and cultural support.

Sunshine Coast Health Centre
- Location: Powell River, British Columbia
- Website: www.sunshinecoasthealthcentre.ca
- Private, non-12-step addiction and trauma treatment facility for men, specializing in both mental health and addiction recovery.

Gibson House Recovery Centre
- Location: Winnipeg, Manitoba
- Website: www.gibsonrecoverycentre.ca
- Offers residential treatment programs for men dealing with addiction and mental health disorders.

Ledgehill Treatment Centre
- Location: Lawrencetown, Nova Scotia
- Website: www.ledgehill.com
- Provides holistic inpatient rehabilitation for both men and women in a retreat-style setting.

Bellwood Health Services (Edgewood Health Network)
- Location: Toronto, Ontario
- Website: www.edgewoodhealthnetwork.com
- Offers inpatient and outpatient addiction treatment programs, with a holistic focus on addiction recovery.

Homewood Health Centre
- Location: Guelph, Ontario
- Website: www.homewoodhealth.com
- One of Canada's largest mental health and addiction treatment centers, offering residential rehab programs.

Pine River Institute
- Location: Shelburne, Ontario
- Website: www.pineriverinstitute.com
- A residential treatment center for adolescents struggling with addiction, integrating mental health and educational support.

Renascent
- Location: Toronto, Ontario
- Website: www.renascent.ca
- Offers 12-step based inpatient and outpatient rehab programs with a focus on spiritual healing.

USA: Rehab Centres

Cliffside Malibu
- Location: Malibu, California
- Website: www.cliffsidemalibu.com

- Known for its luxury residential treatment facility, offering holistic recovery programs and evidence-based care.

Promises Treatment Centers
- Locations: California and Texas
- Website: www.promises.com
- Well-known for luxury inpatient rehab programs and personalized treatment for substance use and mental health disorders.

Silver Hill Hospital
- Location: New Canaan, Connecticut
- Website: www.silverhillhospital.org
- Non-profit psychiatric hospital that provides residential treatment for substance use and co-occurring mental health conditions.

The Recovery Village
- Locations: Florida, Colorado, Ohio, Washington
- Website: www.therecoveryvillage.com
- Offers inpatient and outpatient care with a focus on co-occurring mental health conditions and addiction treatment.

Caron Treatment Centers
- Locations: Pennsylvania, Florida, and across the U.S.
- Website: www.caron.org
- Offers personalized addiction treatment and behavioral health programs, including treatment for teens and families.

Mount Sinai Wellness Center
- Location: Dahlonega, Georgia
- Website: www.mtsinaiwellness.com
- Offers a private and scenic setting for inpatient rehab with a focus on holistic healing and evidence-based therapies.

Timberline Knolls
- Location: Lemont, Illinois
- Website: www.timberlineknolls.com
- A residential treatment center for women, offering programs for addiction, eating disorders, and trauma.

Seabrook
- Location: Bridgeton, New Jersey

- Website: www.seabrook.org
- Specializes in inpatient rehab and family-focused addiction treatment programs.

Caron Treatment Centers
- Locations: Pennsylvania, Florida, and across the U.S.
- Website: www.caron.org
- Offers personalized addiction treatment and behavioral health programs, including treatment for teens and families.

The Ranch Pennsylvania
- Location: Wrightsville, Pennsylvania
- Website: www.recoveryranchpa.com
- Provides trauma-focused addiction treatment programs in a tranquil rural setting.

Cumberland Heights
- Location: Nashville, Tennessee
- Website: www.cumberlandheights.org
- A well-established non-profit treatment facility offering a range of inpatient and outpatient services.

Promises Treatment Centers
- Locations: California and Texas
- Website: www.promises.com
- Well-known for luxury inpatient rehab programs and personalized treatment for substance use and mental health disorders.

Other (USA-Affiliated)

Crossroads Centre Antigua
- Location: Antigua (USA-affiliated)
- Website: www.crossroadsantigua.org
- Founded by musician Eric Clapton, Crossroads offers high-end treatment for addiction in a serene Caribbean environment.

Acknowledgments

We would like to thank the following organizations and individuals for their support in Healing & Hope:

Luke Wiltshire Addiction Consultant
Healing and Hope for Families
Pam Rader at Shift Labs
Rusti L Lehay of Word Quest
Virginia L Lehay
Pharmasave #276 Kelowna Downtown
The Core Centre for Health
Space Centre Storage
Sena College of Massage Therapy
Alexander Security Inc.

www.addictionrecoverystories.com

www.ingramcontent.com/pod-product-compliance
Lightning Source LLC
Chambersburg PA
CBHW030549080526
44585CB00012B/317